Janella's SUPER NATURAL FOODS

JANELLA PURCELL

ALLEN&UNWIN

SYDNEY · MELBOURNE · AUCKLAND · LONDON

This book is intended as a cookbook and a source of information, not as a medical reference book. The reader is advised not to attempt self-treatment for serious or long-term problems without consulting a health professional.

Neither the author nor the publisher can be held responsible for any adverse reaction to the recipes, recommendations and instructions contained in the book, and the use of any ingredients is entirely at the reader's own risk.

Measure guide: We have used 20 ml (4 teaspoon) tablespoon measures. If you are using a 15 ml (3 teaspoon) tablespoon, add an extra teaspoon of the ingredient for each tablespoon specified.

Acknowledgements

For their generous support of this book, special thanks to Lifestream, Vitamix and Loving Earth. Thanks also to these Bangalow retail stores: Little Peach, The Corner Store, Island Luxe and Heath's Old Wares.

First published in 2014
Copyright © Janella Purcell 2014

Allen & Unwin
83 Alexander Street
Crows Nest NSW 2065
Australia
Phone: (61 2)8425 0100
Email: info@allenandunwin.com
Web: www.allenandunwin.com

Cataloguing-in-Publication details are available
from the National Library of Australia
www.trove.nla.gov.au

ISBN 978 1 74331 901 7

Photography by Heath Missen (www.theleftlane.com.au)
Set in 11/13 pt Bailey Sans ITC by Liz Seymour, Seymour Designs
Colour reproduction by Megan Ellis
Printed and bound in China by Hangtai Printing Company Ltd

10 9 8 7 6 5 4 3 2

CONTENTS

INTRODUCTION

SUPER NATURAL FOODS FOR PERMANENT AND SUSTAINABLE WELLNESS

Since *Janella's Wholefood Kitchen* was published in 2012, my travels have been many and varied. And as usual the recipes in this book have found their roots in many different cuisines and cultures – Italian, Japanese, Indian, the Middle East and South East Asia – and some from our own exciting new way of eating and cooking here in Australia.

I'm really excited by different cuisines and look out for different techniques, ingredients and recipes that I can modify into a 'Janella' recipe. When I eat something or watch it being made I'm always thinking: I'll just swap the white sugar for coconut palm sugar, the palm oil for coconut oil, the ghee for olive oil, or I'll use beetroot juice instead of food colouring. That way we can still enjoy many of the dishes we have come to love but in an ethical, healthy and environmentally sound way. What could be better than that? No guilt, on any level.

A lot has happened in the world of nutrition since my last book. Coconut is now a health food, raw chocolate is one of the best things you can eat, and green smoothies are the hippest accessory around. But this influx of new information and ingredients also causes a lot of confusion. Add to that the many new 'diets' – such as high protein/low carb, or no sugar – we read about every day and the information battlefield only increases. Now we're second-guessing everything we put into our mouths. No wonder most people don't know what's good for them.

The answer, as always, is Keep It Simple. If we eat food in its natural state – and mostly plant food – that's a great start. Add to that fermented foods and a few superfoods – high in antioxidants and omega 3 fatty acids – and you'll have achieved a pretty amazing diet.

To ensure your continuing good nutrition, the quantity of processed and refined foods you eat should be reduced if not eliminated altogether, as should trans fatty acids such as margarine and refined vegetable oils.

I spend most of my days working with food and sharing my knowledge with clients in my naturopathic clinics and at demonstrations and events. The importance of sustainability has become a vital and intrinsic part of what I do and say about our eating choices and the growing of our food. I'd like to share with you a few examples of how each of us can make a difference.

Palm oil is a crop that has been used extensively in processed food to extend its shelf life. This is at great cost to the wildlife that depends upon the rainforests, which are being destroyed in order to plant palm trees. Because of this, I decided not to buy anything containing palm oil or palm sugar. Palm oil is often described as *vegetable oil* in the ingredients. You'll find it also in many cosmetics.

I've definitely seen an increase in digestive problems in my clients and have wondered if it's related to the genetically modified (GMO) crops being grown in Australia today. We're now trialling GM wheat, pineapple, papayas, barley and sugarcane. These products have been modified for insect resistance, herbicide tolerance, colour, oil production, sugar composition, flowering and fruit development. Gene technology research is now being conducted in Australia on bananas, rice and corn. Wheat itself is not yet a genetically modified organism, but evidence suggests that other frequently consumed foods – such as soy and corn – may help explain the recent increase in gluten-related disorders. My advice, and my practice, is to buy organic and GMO-free whenever buying packaged foods.

Environmentally there's a real problem with eating the amount of meat we do, but so many of us are convinced we can't cook a satisfying meal without it. I believe that it's wasteful and irresponsible to squander our precious environmental resources on a luxury item like meat, if only because it's estimated that it takes 1000 litres of water to produce a quarter of a kilogram of beef! The more you look into these facts and figures, the more interesting it becomes. If you'd like to investigate further, please look at the website of the Food and Agriculture Organization of the United Nations (FAO) at www.fao.org/about/en/.

This book will help you to create delicious, fantastic and healthy meatless meals for your breakfasts, lunches and dinners. But I'm not dictating that you must cut out meat altogether (although many of us have chosen to do so); I'm suggesting you at least try to cut down. We need to eat more intelligently and that means including more plant food.

All the recipes in this book are vegetarian or vegan – most with variations on how to substitute other ingredients, so you can adapt one meal to suit the whole family. Those less than enthusiastic about vegetarian food will never know that what they're eating is super healthy, super natural and plant-based. Everyone will love these recipes because they're super tasty. If someone in your family eats animal products, you can easily substitute organic chicken or meat where I've used soy products (tofu and tempeh) or legumes. Or meat stocks where I've included veggie stock. It's about eating fewer animal products – and buying the best quality you can afford. I'd really recommend you source organic meat, both for your health and the sustainability of our planet.

Perhaps being a 'flexitarian' is the next step forward for most of us. Eat mostly plant-based foods at home and then be a little flexible when you're out. Fanaticism is not the way to better health; quite the opposite. We want to be friends with our plate, not feel deprived. With an estimated 8 billion people on the planet by 2025, the food of the future needs to be mostly plant-based.

If you'd like to know more about what foods are ethical and sustainable as you shop, and you have a smartphone or tablet, check your app store. I like the Australian Marine Conservation Society's 'Sustainable Seafood Guide', and you'll find ethical shopping apps available too.

KEEPING IT SIMPLE

There are many health and/or environmental factors of which I'd like you to be aware, as well as many alternatives to regularly used ingredients. My advice is to *Swap it!* Milk, oil, sugar, flour, salt, bread, meat – there are many options available now. Simply swap your old unsustainable and unhealthy choices for ones that are good for both you and our planet. Check out the alternatives below and bear them in mind when you're shopping for ingredients.

ANIMAL PRODUCTS

See also Seafood. These are limited in a healthy diet and when you do choose them, buy organic, not just free-range. Otherwise you are consuming many man-made toxins and synthetic oestrogens, not to mention supporting factory farming and GMOs. Some free-range products will be okay but do your research.

BREAD

Sourdough is a great choice because it doesn't (or shouldn't) contain any baker's yeast. Sourdoughs can still be made from white, refined and bleached flour, so check that a wholegrain like spelt, rye, kamut, barley or brown rice has been used. When choosing a gluten-free bread, check it doesn't contain lots of processed ingredients. Bread should be simple.

COCONUT

This is wonderfully healthy for you but if you don't like the flavour or texture, try swapping it for another oil, milk or flour. You could just leave out the flaked, shredded or desiccated coconut or simply use a nut meal instead.

COOKWARE

Avoid non-stick pans. Cast-iron, enamel-coated cast-iron and stainless steel are the best to use.

DAIRY

See also Yoghurt. Fermented dairy products such as kefir, quark and yoghurt are not only easier to digest but also wonderful for stimulating good gut flora and immunity. Goat's products are also anti-inflammatory and easier to digest.

DRIED FRUIT

This is often preserved with a toxic gas called sulphur dioxide, so either buy organic or look for 'sulphur-free' dried fruit.

EGGS

Eggs need to be organic or bio-dynamic, not just free-range. The latter may still be given chemically enhanced feed. In many cases you can use one tablespoon of chia seeds or ground flax mixed with three tablespoons of water in place of an egg.

FERMENTED FOODS

Use a starter like a scoby (symbiotic culture of bacteria and yeast), grains or a mother to start the fermentation process. You can find out how to grow your own starter on the internet. Soy-based fermented foods are miso, tempeh and natto miso; dairy-based fermented foods are kefir, quark and yoghurt. And you can ferment veggies as well – for example, kimchi, sauerkraut and dill pickles.

FLOUR

Unless specified, use any of these – spelt (if not gluten-free), brown rice, amaranth, buckwheat, besan (made from chickpeas), millet or coconut flour, and in some cases almond or any other nut meal.

GMO CROPS

Look for certified organic *and* GMO-free soy and canola in products that contain these crops. Genetically modified food products on sale in Australia and New Zealand, either as a whole food or as an ingredient in a processed food, must have their GM status identified if introduced genetic material or protein is present in the final food. However, there are exceptions:

> foods where GM ingredients are highly refined, such as cooking oils, margarine, sugars, starches, chocolate and baked goods (many processed foods fall into this category);

> foods made at bakeries, restaurants and takeaway outlets;
> foods from animals that eat GM feed; and
> manufacturers who use a wide range of GM food ingredients imported from overseas. These include specific GM varieties of soy beans, corn, rice, potatoes and sugar beet (a cousin of beetroot).

HONEY

Look for organic or at least 'raw' honey, otherwise it has probably been refined – which means filtered – and will therefore be almost devoid of any nutrients or medicinal properties.

JUICES

Avoid fruit juices unless a small amount is needed in a recipe. General rule – juice your veggies and eat your fruit. There's too much fructose and none of the fruit's fibre in fruit juice, and it will also cause a spike in your blood sugar levels.

MILK

Unless specified in the recipe you can use almond, rice, oat, organic soy, coconut, quinoa, hemp, sunflower seed or hazelnut milk. There are so many now available from which you can choose your favourites.

NOODLES

Avoid wheat noodles unless they're made from spelt flour. Instead look for kelp, buckwheat, quinoa, millet, amaranth, organic corn and brown rice noodles.

NUT BUTTERS

Peanuts are heavily sprayed with chemicals, so buy organic peanut butter. Also look out for almond, cashew, pistachio and Brazil nut butters.

OILS

> For high-temperature cooking use unrefined avocado, macadamia, sunflower, coconut or extra virgin olive oil.
> For lower temperature cooking, use any of the above.

- › Keep hemp and flax oil raw.
- › Avoid GMO canola and soy oils.
- › Avoid trans fats like margarine and refined vegetable oils.
- › Avoid palm oil as it is not only destroying the natural habitat of the now endangered orangutan and Sumatran tiger but is also an unsustainable and toxic farming practice.
- › Buy or store oils in dark, glass bottles.

ORGANIC FOOD
If you can buy organic, then do it. I think it will be the best move you've ever made towards better health. Look for a stamp from a certifying body such as Australian Organics or OGA in Australia, or Ecocert in North America.

PASTA
Spelt pasta is widely available these days, and a great alternative to regular wheat pasta if you're not gluten-free. Also look out for organic mung, black and soy bean pasta that is organic and gluten-free.

PEPPER
Use cracked black pepper unless specified otherwise.

PLASTIC
Plastic containers may contain toxic chemicals, BPA and phthalates. To be sure, I always use glass containers or plates on top of bowls of leftovers to store food.

QUINOA
Look for quinoa that is Australian-grown, as our appetite for this wonderful grain is pushing the price up, making it unaffordable for the Bolivians, who grow it and use it as a staple food.

RICE
Buy organic or pesticide-free brown rice. It is much softer, fluffier and easier to digest than regular brown rice.

SALT
Use Murray River, Celtic, Himalayan or Maldon salt, and use river or unrefined salt in preference to rock salt.

SEAFOOD
Make it sustainable or don't buy it at all. Check the Australian Marine Conservation Society website or their app. The only fresh salmon available in Australia is farmed and also fed GMO pellets, so buy tinned wild salmon from Alaska – line- and pole-caught – and in a tin with BPA-free lining. Avoid all tuna as they are over-fished and too high in the heavy metal, mercury.

SEAWEED
Due to the Fukushima nuclear disaster, avoid any that come from Japan. Look for cleaner, naturally dried seaweeds from Australia, New Zealand and Alaska.

SOY
Soy is a genetically modified crop so buying organic in this case is a must. Fermented soy products like tempeh, miso and natto are easier to digest than tofu and milk. Look for soy milk that is Australian-made and cane sugar-free.

SULPHUR DIOXIDE
This a toxic gas used to preserve food and its colour, and also to extend its shelf life. It has been shown to cause hives and migraines and other allergic reactions as well as contribute to upper respiratory cancers. Check the ingredients of all processed foods, including wine.

SWEETENERS
- › Syrups: use golden syrup, raw agave, maple or rice bran syrup, raw honey or coconut nectar.
- › Granules: use either coconut palm sugar or rapadura (panela) instead of white, raw or brown sugar.

TAHINI

Unless specified otherwise, use hulled tahini. This has been heated so the outer husks of the sesame seed crack open and are then removed, which gives it a milder taste and a lighter colour. If you'd like to keep them or a dish raw, then buy tahini 'unhulled'.

TINS

The metallic lining in tins can contain a toxic chemical called BPA that leaches into the food once the tin is heated and sealed. You can buy BPA-free tins though – check the information on the tin itself.

VINEGAR

Unless I've specified a particular vinegar in a recipe, you can use any type you have to hand – for example, brown rice, coconut, apple cider, balsamic, shaoxing (black Chinese rice wine), raspberry, white or red wine. If you can find a umeboshi vinegar that doesn't come from Japan, where the radioactive fallout from the Fukushima disaster is still a problem, use it to add a sharp saltiness.

WATER

I don't use tap water and don't recommend you do either. Buy a filter for your tap or a jug that filters tap water.

YOGHURT

Please buy full-fat and sugar-free yoghurt. Apart from cow's milk yoghurt, you can also buy sheep's, buffalo, goat's and coconut. Making your own is easy.

RECIPE CODES

As you're choosing which recipes to cook within these pages, you'll see that there are easy-to-identify codes under each recipe title to indicate whether it is dairy-free, gluten-free, grain-free, nut-free, raw, soy-free, vegetarian or vegan. These codes will tell you exactly which dishes you need to choose in order to keep you, your family and friends safe while eating familiar favourites and new taste sensations that will keep you healthy.

DF	Dairy-free
GF	Gluten-free
GrF	Grain-free
NF	Nut-free
R	Raw
SF	Soy-free
V	Vegetarian
VG	Vegan

I hope you enjoy cooking from my new *Super Natural Foods* cookbook. I've loved compiling this collection and look forward to your feedback on my website (janellapurcell.com) or on my Facebook page (www.facebook.com/JanellaPurcell).

Janella Purcell

CHIA BREAKFAST PUDDINGS

DF VG V SF R

What did we do for so long without chia seeds? Certainly we didn't have access to such a great plant source of calcium, omega 3 oils or protein, and I don't think we smiled as much at breakfast (or dessert). Double or triple this recipe so you can enjoy one of these delightful puddings for breakfast on the go, or whenever you have a little sweet craving that needs satisfying. I've used mason jars here.

750 ml (26 fl oz/3 cups) coconut, oat or almond milk

2 tbsp chia seeds

2 tbsp toasted almonds, roughly chopped

2 tbsp hemp seeds

½ cup berries or pomegranate seeds

½ tsp ground cinnamon

1 Divide the ingredients between two 200 ml (7 fl oz) glass jars with lids, then shake well for about 10 seconds. Pop them in the fridge overnight to set the puddings and allow the chia seeds to form their gelatinous texture.

VARIATIONS

The possibilities with the combinations are almost endless. Try adding:

✔ 750 ml (26 fl oz/3 cups) cold-pressed apple juice, then blend with 1 banana, ½ tsp ground cinnamon, 2 tsp raw honey, 2 tbsp toasted almonds and 2 tbsp chia seeds.

✔ ½ cup any puffed grain like quinoa, amaranth or brown rice.

✔ 2 tbsp dried fruit, like goji berries or apricots.

✔ 2 tbsp raw cacao powder or cacao nibs (to give you a chocolate + chia pudding).

✔ 2 tsp maca powder for extra energy.

SUPER GREEN SMOOTHIE

It's easy to design your own smoothie by adding to a liquid base some fruit, veggies, nuts or seeds, oil and a probiotic. If you have a high-speed blender, add some veggies, nuts and seeds to your smoothie, as its powerful motor will give you a lovely smooth texture. If you don't, then leave them out as the texture will be a bit chunky and not so nice. Leave in the hemp and chia seeds and flaxseed meal, as they blend nicely. Try to always include a micro green like spirulina, barley grass or wheatgrass so you have a green smoothie. This will help clean out your liver with each sip. Then finish with a sweetener and a probiotic if desired.

LIQUID BASE

750 ml (26 fl oz/3 cups) base liquid (choose from: oat, rice, quinoa, hemp, soy or raw (unpasteurised) cow's milk, coconut water or water)

FRUIT

1 cup fruit (such as papaya, strawberries, banana, berries, any melon, pear, lime, lemon, dates, goji berries)

VEGGIES

1 cup veggies (such as broccoli, beetroot, cucumber, carrot, baby spinach, cabbage, kale, zucchini)

SUPER NATURAL FOODS

1 tsp each of any or as many of these super natural foods as you like – camu camu powder, gubinge powder, spirulina, wheatgrass, barley grass, pea protein powder, mesquite powder, maca powder, psyllium husks, raw cacao, puffed grains, acai powder, silken tofu for protein and fibre; coconut, hemp, chia seed or flaxseed oil; ground flaxseeds, LSA, hulled or unhulled tahini, chia seeds, hemp seeds, sunflower seeds, sesame seeds, pepitas, raw unsalted nuts

SWEETENER

1 tsp of a sweetener (optional) – raw honey, rice syrup, coconut syrup or pure maple syrup

PROBIOTIC

1 tsp probiotic (optional) – kefir, quark or yoghurt

GREAT PORRIDGE

GF DF VG V SF NF

This recipe shows just how much our nutrition has improved. Say goodbye to microwaved oats with skim milk, brown sugar and a banana, and hi to a bowl full of high nutrient, easy-to-digest goodness. This is a lovely porridge in the cooler months. By letting it soak overnight, you'll shorten the cooking time in the morning and make it more digestible, but it's not essential to do so.

PORRIDGE

55 g (2 oz/½ cup) quinoa flakes, brown rice flakes or fine polenta

1 cinnamon stick or 1 tsp ground cinnamon

1 tbsp grated lemon, lime or orange zest

1 date or 2 dried figs

2 cardamom pods, crushed or ½ tsp ground cardamom

1 tsp grated fresh ginger or ½ tsp ground

1 tsp grated fresh turmeric or ½ tsp ground

1 tbsp chia seeds

1 tbsp goji berries

pinch of unrefined salt

300 ml (10½ fl oz) water or rice milk

2 tsp hemp oil

2 tsp flaxseed oil

TO SERVE

2 tbsp Coconut yoghurt (page 152)

1 tsp syrup or granule sweetener or 2 tbsp Stewed nutty fruit (page 182) (optional)

1   Mix all the porridge ingredients together in a saucepan, cover and place in the fridge overnight.

2   The next morning, pop the pan on the stove and bring to the boil over medium–low heat. Reduce the heat to low, then simmer for 5 minutes, stirring continuously. You may need more water, so add as necessary.

3   Serve drizzled with the sweetener or a dollop each of stewed nutty fruit and the coconut yoghurt.

VARIATIONS

✓ You can also use amaranth, millet or oat flakes.

✓ Try coconut water instead of water or rice milk.

✓ Leave out the dried fruit and use a sliced banana (added in the morning) or ½ cup frozen berries instead.

✓ Use 2 tbsp goat's, sheep's or cow's yoghurt instead of coconut yoghurt.

FUL MEDAMES

GF DF VG V SF NF

Literally meaning 'stewed dried beans', Ful is a common breakfast in the Middle East, and we've recently started catching on. Ful is made up of broad beans, spices, sometimes a boiled egg, and pieces of flatbread. It's traditionally made with dried beans that require hours of preparation, but I've written a modern day Ful recipe so we can enjoy it more often, as it's faster to put together. Of course Ful isn't limited to the morning – it can be enjoyed at any time of the day or night.

310 g (11 oz/2 cups) frozen or
   1 × 400 g (14 oz) BPA-free tin broad
   beans

2–4 garlic cloves, crushed (optional)

splash of water

2 tbsp lemon juice

2 tbsp olive oil

½ tsp ground cumin

½ tsp unrefined salt

1 tsp paprika, sweet or smoked

lots of chopped flat-leaf parsley,
   to serve

Flatbread (page 134), to serve

1   Drain and rinse the tinned beans or, if using frozen, prepare according to the instructions on the packet. You may need to peel them.

2   Then pop them in a frying pan over medium–high heat with the garlic and water and cook for a couple of minutes. Once the beans are hot, roughly mash with a fork, then spoon onto a plate.

3   In a small bowl, mix together the lemon juice, olive oil, cumin and salt.

4   Pour the dressing over the beans and mix well. Sprinkle on the paprika and serve with loads of parsley and the flatbread.

VARIATIONS

✓ Tinned broad beans can be difficult to find, but chickpeas, navy or kidney beans are great alternatives.

✓ Use only half the broad beans, serve on a bed of Hummus (page 160) and garnish with chickpeas, chopped parsley, sliced onion and a boiled egg. For 2 people.

✓ Try it with cubes of goat's feta, olives and sliced cucumbers.

✓ Replace the flatbread with 185 g (6½ oz/1 cup) cooked quinoa.

✓ It's lovely with Tahini dressing (page 160), boiled eggs, sliced tomato and raw onion wedges.

✓ Add a dollop of quark and a fermented veggie, such as sauerkraut or dill pickles.

SUPER NATURAL BIRCHER MUESLI

GF DF VG V SF

I love to recommend this gluten- and dairy-free Bircher muesli to my clients as it has everything in one bowl, it's quick to prepare in the morning and it is so easy to digest. To keep it raw, use raw nuts and pepitas instead of my recommended toasted, or leave them out altogether. Make lots, as it will last for about a week in the fridge.

55 g (2 oz/½ cup) quinoa flakes

2 tsp chia seeds

2 tsp hemp seeds

1 tbsp goji berries

35 g (1¼ oz/½ cup) shredded or fresh coconut

1 tbsp grated lemon zest

1 granny smith apple or pear, grated

500 ml (17 fl oz/2 cups) coconut water

2 tbsp any toasted nuts (such as pecans, walnuts or pistachios)

TO SERVE

200 g (7 oz/¾ cup) Coconut yoghurt (page 152)

1 cup any chopped fruit (such as apple, pear, peach or berries)

2 tbsp pepitas, toasted

1   In a large bowl, combine all the muesli ingredients. Cover and leave in the fridge overnight. In the morning stir through the yoghurt and top with the fruit and seeds.

VARIATIONS

✔ Use cold-pressed pear or apple juice instead of the coconut water.

✔ Serve with 2 tsp hemp, flaxseed, coconut or chia oil.

✔ You can use any toasted seeds like sunflower, sesame or poppy to garnish.

✔ Serve with Stewed nutty fruit (page 182).

✔ For a nice garnish, add 2 tbsp flaked almonds.

✔ Use cow's, sheep's or goat's yoghurt instead of the coconut yoghurt but note it will no longer be vegan or dairy-free.

✔ Try sultanas – or any dried fruit – instead of the goji berries.

QUINOA BREAKFAST PATTIES

GF DF V SF NF

I usually have leftover quinoa in the fridge, which makes preparing this breakfast super-quick.

2 tsp olive or coconut oil

2 eggs

185 g (6½ oz/1 cup) cooked quinoa

2 tbsp chopped herbs (such as chives, flat-leaf parsley, basil or coriander)

pinch of unrefined salt

1   Heat a heavy-based frying pan over medium–high heat and add the oil.

2   In a small bowl, whisk together the eggs, quinoa, herbs and salt, then pour into the pan. Using a spatula, shape the mixture into a round and cook for 1–2 minutes until the underside is brown, then flip and cook for another minute or so until both sides are golden. Cut in half to serve.

VARIATIONS

✔ Use millet instead of quinoa, or a mixture of both.

✔ Add 1 tbsp soft goat's feta to the egg before whisking, leaving out the salt.

✔ Spread 1 tsp soft goat's cheese on top, then sprinkle with a few hemp seeds.

✔ Use 'flax eggs' instead of eggs. For each **Flax egg**, dissolve 1 tsp flaxseed meal in 2–3 tbsp water.

✔ Use leftover Ancient grains (page 130) instead of quinoa.

TEMPEH IN NORI WITH ROCKET AND AVOCADO

GF DF VG V NF

For the person who likes a savoury start (or middle or end) to their day, you're going to just love this. Personally, it's one of my favourites. Tempeh is a plant protein so will keep you nicely full for longer, and being fermented and loaded with fibre, it will be of great benefit to your immune system and digestive tract.

2 tsp coconut oil

100 g (3½ oz) tempeh, cut into 5 slices

1 tsp tamari

2 sheets of toasted nori

5 thin slices of avocado

1 spring onion, thinly sliced

1 small handful of rocket leaves

1 tsp hemp seeds

1   Heat the oil in a heavy-based frying pan over medium–high heat. Add your tempeh and cook for about 2 minutes on each side until golden and crunchy. Drain on paper towel then drizzle with the tamari.

2   Lay your 2 nori sheets beside each other, shiny side down, on a work surface. Lay 2–3 avocado slices on each sheet, about 2.5 cm (1 in) from the edge nearest to you. Next top with the spring onion, rocket, slices of tempeh and hemp seeds. Roll up firmly. Cut in half to serve.

VARIATIONS

✔ Try spreading 1 tsp whole-egg or organic soy mayo, 1 tsp dijon mustard or miso paste on each nori sheet.

✔ Use baby spinach leaves instead of the rocket.

✔ Add slices of tomato.

✔ Squash on leftover steamed or baked pumpkin or grilled zucchini.

✔ Try different seeds, such as toasted sunflower or sesame seeds or pepitas.

✔ Use a One-egg omelette (page 12) instead of the tempeh.

ONE-EGG OMELETTE

GF V SF NF

I've included many variations here, as there's just so much you can do with this crepe-like omelette. Once you make this, you'll wonder why you haven't before. I find this is the easiest way to digest eggs. I have doubled the recipe to make two omelettes and filled these with the potato, saffron and quark variation below.

2 eggs

1 tbsp chopped fresh herbs (such as tarragon, flat-leaf parsley, dill or basil)

2 tbsp coconut or olive oil

1 In a small bowl, whisk together your eggs and herbs.

2 Heat your frying pan over medium heat, then add 1 tablespoon of the oil. Pour half the egg mixture into your pan and use a fork to spread it around so it's quite thin and round. Allow to bubble up and brown a little, then flip and cook on the other side for about 30–60 seconds until golden on this side. Fold in half and serve. Repeat with the remaining oil and the egg mixture.

VARIATIONS

✓ Add a pinch of unrefined salt.

✓ After the first flip, sprinkle on 1 tbsp goat's cheese or quark.

✓ For a more substantial brunch dish, boil 1 roughly diced waxy potato with ½ tsp saffron until tender. Season with ½ tsp each of unrefined salt and cracked black pepper and scatter on a handful of chopped baby spinach. When cooked, add 1 tsp lemon juice and a dollop of quark or yoghurt. Stir with a wooden spoon, spread it over half the omelette, then fold. Fold again to create a fan shape.

✓ Serve in Flatbread (page 134) with a scrape of avocado or 1 tsp soft goat's cheese or quark.

✓ Place 2 slices of smoked salmon on top of the omelette after the first flip.

✓ Serve with a drizzle of tamari.

✓ After the first flip, fill with a handful of leafy greens or sautéed kale, then fold in half.

✓ Sprinkle with 2 tsp hemp seeds and shredded basil or mint leaves.

✓ For a bigger brekkie, fill your omelette with a few tbsp of Seven-spiced baked beans (page 100), a couple of avocado slices and Tahini dressing (page 160).

SHAKSHUKA

GF DF V SF NF

Here's another Middle Eastern breakfast to add to your morning routine. I highly recommend you make a few batches of this tasty sauce and have it on hand in the freezer in portions, as it's just so versatile. Use it on pizza, as a pasta sauce, in toasted wraps or sandwiches, as a side to your protein at dinner, mix it through some legumes or ladle it over some cooked grains or quinoa – or enjoy just like this. Serve it with a drizzle of Tahini dressing (page 160) or some quark or a dollop of labne.

½ tsp cumin seeds

3 tbsp olive oil

1 onion, sliced

1 small red and 1 small yellow capsicum, sliced

1 tbsp coconut palm sugar or rapadura

1 bay leaf

1 tbsp thyme sprigs, chopped

½ cup mixed flat-leaf parsley and coriander leaves, plus extra to serve

3 ripe tomatoes, roughly chopped

½ tsp saffron threads (optional but yummy)

¼ tsp cayenne pepper

unrefined salt and cracked black pepper

about 250 ml (9 fl oz/1 cup) water

4 eggs

1   In a large, preferably cast-iron, frying pan, toast the cumin seeds over low heat for 1 minute – shaking the pan – until they become fragrant and change colour slightly. Then add the oil and onion and sauté for 5 minutes. Next, increase the heat to medium–high, then stir in the capsicum, sugar, bay leaf and herbs and cook for 5–10 minutes.

2   Add the tomato, saffron, if using, cayenne pepper and salt and pepper, and simmer over low heat for about 10 minutes until it is intense in flavour and the consistency of a chunky pasta sauce. You may need to add some water if the mixture is too thick. (You can freeze this base for 3 months if you like.)

3   Remove the bay leaf then, using a spoon, make 4 holes, each about 10 cm (4 in) wide, in the mixture. Carefully break an egg into each hole. (You can also divide the mixture between 4 individual smaller pans if you have them – gorgeous.) Cover with a lid and reduce the heat to as low as it will go and gently heat for about 10 minutes, depending on how you like your eggs. Alternatively, you can bake the shakshuka at 180°C (350°F/Gas 4) for about 5 minutes, or until the eggs are set.

4   Sprinkle with the extra parsley and coriander and place on the table ready to eat.

SUPER NATURAL START

GF V SF

Packed with protein – thanks to the hemp, millet, nuts and quinoa – for sustained energy, this is an easy and nutritious way to start the day. The coconut is wonderful for weight loss, is antifungal and makes for glowing skin and hair. This is also a nice thing to eat mid-afternoon to avoid being starving at dinnertime. Make it in the morning, pop it in a jar or your BPA-free lunchbox and take it to work, or leave it in the fridge at home, and by the afternoon the goji berries will be soft.

390 g (13¾ oz/1½ cups) plain or
   coconut yoghurt

2 tbsp mixed seeds (such as sunflower,
   sesame, hemp and chia seeds,
   pepitas or flaxseed meal)

15 g (½ oz/½ cup) puffed quinoa,
   brown rice, millet or amaranth

2 tbsp coconut flakes

2 tbsp goji berries

2 tbsp Stewed nutty fruit (page 182)

1   Place the yoghurt in your bowl, jar or lunchbox, then top with everything else and stir. Serve.

VARIATIONS

✓ You can use fresh fruit instead of the stewed nutty fruit.

✓ For a sweeter option, add 1 tsp rice, maple, raw agave or coconut syrup.

✓ For a nice crunch and a hit of antioxidants, add 2 tbsp cacao nibs.

✓ Finish with a drizzle of hemp, chia, flaxseed or coconut oil.

LUNCH

INDONESIAN SALAD

GF DF VG V GrF

This peanut sauce is amazing. Be sure you buy organic peanuts as these 'groundnuts' are heavily sprayed with chemicals. Make lots of the sauce and freeze it in portions for up to three months. In its home country of Indonesia, you'll find gado gado is served with a halved boiled egg, but you can leave it out, as I often do, to make this dish vegan.

250 g (9 oz/2 cups) sliced string or snake beans

230 g (8½ oz/2 cups) bean sprouts

100 g (3½ oz/1 cup) sliced snow peas

2 cups chopped Asian greens (such as bok choy or choy sum)

1 carrot, julienned

1 zucchini, cut into half moons

300 g (10½ oz) tempeh, cut into 8 × 1-cm (½-in) slices

1 tbsp tamari, plus extra to drizzle

1 tbsp avocado or coconut oil

70 g (2½ oz/½ cup) roasted peanuts, skin off, crushed

15 g (½ oz/½ cup) Thai basil or coriander leaves

PEANUT SAUCE

2 tbsp coconut oil

4 garlic cloves

4 red Asian shallots, thinly sliced

2 long red chillies, halved lengthways, deseeded and sliced

1 tbsp grated fresh or 1 tsp ground turmeric

2 kaffir lime leaves, thinly sliced

260 g (9¼ oz/1 cup) peanut butter

125 g (4½ oz/½ cup) tamarind pulp

tamari or fish sauce, to taste

1   Steam or blanch your veggies separately until just tender. Drain and set aside.

2   Marinate the tempeh slices in the tamari and set aside for a few minutes.

3   For the sauce, heat the oil in a heavy-based frying pan over medium–high heat, then add the garlic, shallot, chilli and turmeric and cook for another minute or until fragrant.

4   Transfer to a mortar, blender or food processor, add the kaffir lime leaves and peanut butter and grind with a pestle or process to a coarse paste, gradually adding the tamarind pulp and enough warm water to make a paste the consistency of hummus. Taste for seasoning. Add the tamari or fish sauce and taste again.

5   Grill or pan-fry your tempeh in a little oil until golden on both sides. Drain on paper towel, then drizzle with a little tamari.

6   To serve, divide the veggies between each serving plate, then add enough sauce to cover but not drown them. Top with the tempeh and peanuts and finish with basil or coriander leaves.

VARIATIONS

✓   For the kids, leave out the chilli in the sauce.

✓   Add 1 tsp dried shrimp paste (belachan) with the garlic and shallot to the sauce, or add 2 tsp fish sauce to the peanut sauce.

✓   Serve with barbecued tofu, fish, chicken or meat threaded onto skewers.

FRESH SPRING ROLLS WITH PINEAPPLE TERIYAKI SAUCE

GF DF VG V SF NF

I realise these rice paper wrappers are made from white rice (won't it be great when we can get them made from brown rice?) but sometimes it's fine. Besides, they're such a light thing to eat, especially prepared this way. Again, I have included many variations as they lend themselves to so many flavours and ingredients. Try this delicious sauce with other dishes as well.

4 large rice paper wrappers

½ avocado, sliced

4 tbsp julienned Lebanese cucumber

1 small carrot, grated

1 small zucchini, julienned or grated

80 g (2¾ oz/½ cup) finely diced pineapple

PINEAPPLE TERIYAKI SAUCE

40 g (1½ oz/¼ cup) roughly chopped pineapple

1 tbsp ponzu sauce

1 tsp lime juice

1 tsp grated fresh ginger

1   For the sauce, put all the ingredients in a food processor and blitz until you have a smooth consistency. Transfer to a bowl, cover and place in the fridge until you're ready to serve.

2   Meanwhile, place the rice paper wrappers, one at a time, in a shallow bowl of hot water. Leave them in there, swirling them around, for about 30 seconds, then place them on a clean work surface. Divide the avocado slices between the sheets and place about a third of the way up from the side closest to you. Top with the other veggies and the pineapple. Drizzle on a little sauce, then roll up, tucking in the ends as you go. Cut in half and serve with the remaining sauce.

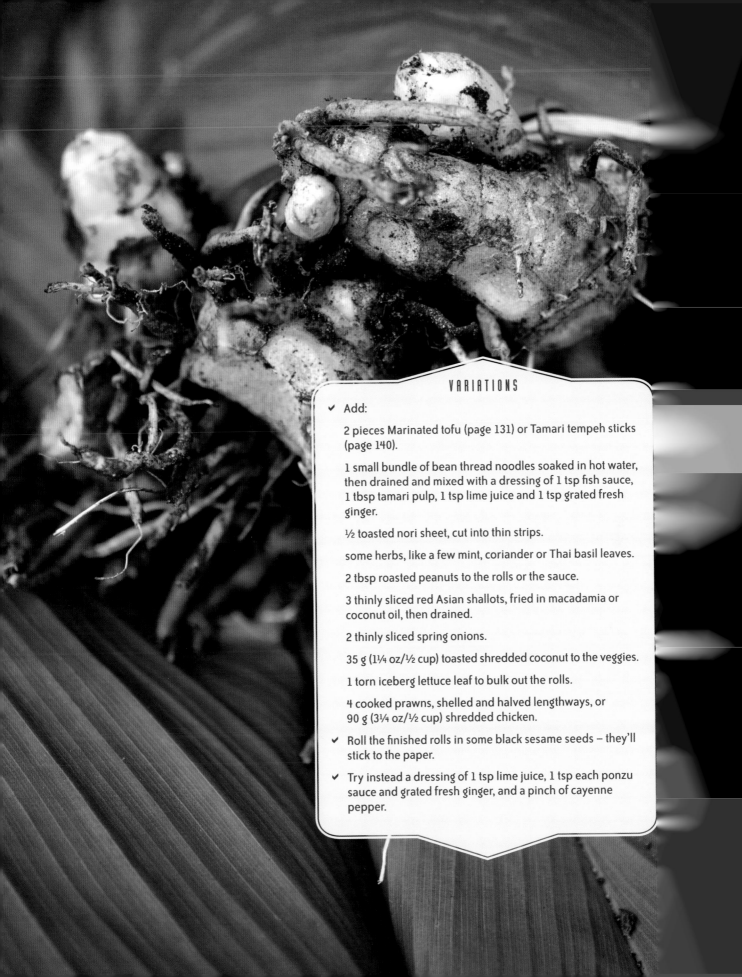

VARIATIONS

✔ Add:

2 pieces Marinated tofu (page 131) or Tamari tempeh sticks (page 140).

1 small bundle of bean thread noodles soaked in hot water, then drained and mixed with a dressing of 1 tsp fish sauce, 1 tbsp tamari pulp, 1 tsp lime juice and 1 tsp grated fresh ginger.

½ toasted nori sheet, cut into thin strips.

some herbs, like a few mint, coriander or Thai basil leaves.

2 tbsp roasted peanuts to the rolls or the sauce.

3 thinly sliced red Asian shallots, fried in macadamia or coconut oil, then drained.

2 thinly sliced spring onions.

35 g (1¼ oz/½ cup) toasted shredded coconut to the veggies.

1 torn iceberg lettuce leaf to bulk out the rolls.

4 cooked prawns, shelled and halved lengthways, or 90 g (3¼ oz/½ cup) shredded chicken.

✔ Roll the finished rolls in some black sesame seeds – they'll stick to the paper.

✔ Try instead a dressing of 1 tsp lime juice, 1 tsp each ponzu sauce and grated fresh ginger, and a pinch of cayenne pepper.

PROTEIN-PACKED LENTIL LOAF

GF DF V

It's super-easy and tasty so it's likely to become another staple. Add or leave out whatever you like or have or don't have in the pantry. As with most of my recipes, there are no rules.

1 tsp–1 tbsp olive oil

1 onion, diced

1–2 garlic cloves, finely chopped

2 celery stalks, diced

1 carrot, grated

1 zucchini, grated

90 g (3¼ oz/1 cup) chopped Swiss brown or button mushrooms

1 × 400 g (14 oz) BPA-free tin brown lentils, drained

1 × 180 g (6½ oz) block firm or soft tofu, mashed with a fork

100 g (3½ oz/1 cup) almond meal

50 g (1¾ oz/ ⅓ cup) chia seeds

15 g (½ oz/½ cup) finely chopped flat-leaf parsley

1 tbsp finely chopped thyme

185 g (6½ oz/1 cup) cooked quinoa

4 eggs, beaten

2 handfuls of leafy dark greens (such as English spinach, kale or silverbeet)

50 g (1¾ oz/1 cup) chopped mixed herbs (such as basil, chives, coriander, mint)

unrefined salt or tamari and cracked black pepper

Tahini dressing (page 160), to serve

green salad, to serve

1. Preheat the oven to 180°C (350°F/Gas 4). Line a 20-cm × 30-cm (8-in × 12-in) loaf tin with baking paper and use a little olive oil to help it stick.

2. In a large frying pan over medium heat, sauté your onion in the oil for 1 minute or so until it starts to soften and change colour, then stir in the garlic and cook for another minute until the onion is translucent. Add the veggies and sauté for another minute until starting to soften.

3. Remove the pan from the heat, then mix in the rest of the ingredients and season.

4. Using wet hands or a spatula, press the mixture into the prepared tin or pan. Bake for about 15–20 minutes until it starts to change colour on the top. Cool slightly, then slice and serve with the Tahini dressing and a green salad.

VARIATIONS

✓ Change the flavour by adding different spices and herbs with the onion. Try 1 tsp ground cumin, sweet or smoked paprika, chopped oregano or curry powder; 2 tsp each of fresh grated or 1 tsp ground turmeric or ginger; 1 tsp cayenne pepper will give it a kick of heat.

✓ You can use any legumes or lentils or some mashed tempeh instead of the brown lentils.

✓ If you're not gluten-free, add 75 g (2½ oz/½ cup) spelt flour, which is high in protein. It will give you a firmer slice.

✓ 1 tbsp tomato paste will make the slice richer in flavour.

✓ Add 1 tbsp each of pepitas, sunflower and sesame seeds.

TOASTED MISO, TAHINI AND QUINOA ROLL-UPS

DF VG V NF

These are great for a party. You can make them ahead of time and when you're ready for them, pop them into a sandwich press to toast. The nori sheets keep the bread from going soggy – but are not essential to include – and the quinoa bulks them out to make quite substantial little rolls. For gluten-free rolls, use gluten-free flatbread.

185 g (6½ oz/1 cup) cooked quinoa

3 handfuls of baby spinach leaves

2 spring onions, finely chopped

6 pieces of Flatbread (page 134)

3 toasted nori sheets, cut in half (optional)

1 lemon, cut into wedges

MISO DRESSING

2 tbsp shiro miso

90 g (3¼ oz/⅓ cup) hulled tahini

2 tsp ginger juice (squeezed from a 5-cm (2-in) piece of grated fresh ginger)

1–2 tbsp lemon juice

1   In a small bowl, make the miso dressing by mixing together the miso, tahini, ginger and lemon juice. You will probably need to add a little water to make it the consistency of runny yoghurt.

2   In a separate bowl, mix together the quinoa, miso dressing, spinach and spring onion.

3   Spread all the flatbreads on a bench then, on the edge closest to you, top each with half a sheet of nori. Spread about 2 tbsp of the quinoa mixture on each nori sheet about 5 cm (2 in) from the edge nearest you. Roll up fairly firmly into a cigar shape.

4   Toast the roll-ups in a preheated sandwich press until just crisp. Cut in half on an angle, then place the roll-ups on a platter and serve with the lemon wedges.

VARIATIONS

✔ Place 150 g (5½ oz) roughly chopped flathead fillets or chicken in a shallow bowl in a bamboo steamer over simmering water and cover. Steam the fish for 3–4 minutes until it easily breaks apart but is still a little undercooked. The chicken will take 6–8 minutes. Cool slightly, then shred and gently stir into the miso dressing.

✔ Use steamed kale or rocket instead of the baby spinach, and millet or Ancient grains (page 130) instead of the quinoa.

✔ To the quinoa mixture, add: 1 tbsp grated lemon, orange or lime zest; or 25 g (1 oz/½ cup) chopped coriander, basil and/or mint leaves; or 1 cup mashed firm or soft tofu.

HAZELNUT AND HERB PASTA SALAD

GF DF VG V SF

This is a beautiful pasta salad to serve at room temperature. It'll take you only a few minutes to prepare and the addition of the truffle or hazelnut oil makes all the difference. A bottle of either of these heavenly oils will last you ages as you only need a little.

4 tbsp extra virgin olive oil

1 brown onion or 2 large French shallots, finely diced

2 garlic cloves, crushed

100 g (3½ oz/2 cups) roughly chopped mixed herbs (such as basil, coriander, mint, chives or fennel tips)

1 tbsp grated lemon or orange zest

2 tsp apple cider vinegar

1 tsp unrefined salt, or to taste

1 tbsp hazelnut or truffle oil, plus extra to serve

1 × 200 g (7 oz) packet black bean or mung bean pasta

1 tbsp preserved lemon, thinly sliced

130 g (4¾ oz/1 cup) roughly chopped toasted hazelnuts

1   Heat the olive oil in a large frying pan over low heat. Add the onion or shallot and garlic and gently sauté, stirring occasionally, for 10 minutes until translucent. Try not to let them change colour.

2   Place your herbs in a bowl then, stirring constantly, add the sautéed onion and garlic mixture, the zest, vinegar and salt. Drizzle in the hazelnut or truffle oil. Taste and adjust the seasoning.

3   Meanwhile, put a large saucepan of water on to boil and cook your pasta according to the packet instructions. Drain well, reserving some of the cooking water, and return to the pan. Add just a little of the reserved water to keep the pasta moist.

4   Pour the herb sauce over the pasta and toss gently. Finish with the preserved lemon.

5   Serve the pasta on a beautiful platter and garnish with the hazelnuts and a drizzle of the hazelnut or truffle oil. If you're making the salad ahead of time, leave the garnish off until you're ready to serve.

VARIATIONS

✓   For a creamy dressing, use just a splash of vinegar and add 390 g (13¾ oz/1½ cups) plain yoghurt or quark.

✓   Use other vinegars, like balsamic, raspberry, brown rice or red wine.

✓   Try Broccoli and mint pesto (page 55) instead of the herbs and hazelnuts.

FANTASTIC VEGGIE FRITTERS

GF DF VG V NF

I make these or a variation of these a couple of times a week. They are super-yummy, quick to prepare, highly nutritious and freeze well. Everyone loves them and they are especially great in kids' lunchboxes – or yours. Use whatever veggies or legume you like. Make double or triple the amount and freeze the fritters for up to three months.

3 tbsp coconut or olive oil

1 small onion or leek, pale part only, washed well, diced

1 tbsp finely chopped coriander stems

1 garlic clove, crushed

1 tsp each grated fresh ginger and turmeric

1 corn cob, kernels removed

125 g (4½ oz/1 cup) grated sweet potato

1 zucchini, grated and squeezed dry

1 tbsp chia seeds

1½ cups dried cooked navy beans or 1 × 400 g (14 oz) BPA-free tin drained navy beans

25 g (1 oz/½ cup) chopped mixed herbs (such as flat-leaf parsley, mint, dill, basil or coriander)

2 tsp unrefined salt or tamari, or to taste

45 g (1½ oz/¼ cup) brown rice flour

1 In a heavy-based frying pan, heat 1 tablespoon of the oil over medium heat, add your onion or leek and the coriander stems and sauté for 1 minute until translucent. Next, add the garlic, ginger and turmeric and stir for a few seconds. Then stir in all the veggies and the chia seeds, mixing well to coat everything in the oil. Remove from the heat.

2 Place the navy beans in a food processor and blitz for a few seconds. Now add the veggie mixture, herbs and salt or tamari. Turn the motor off then add the flour and pulse until you have a firm mixture. (You can also do this step by hand, using a fork to mash the beans.)

3 With wet hands, divide the mixture into 12 and roll into balls about the size of a large walnut, then flatten into a patty.

4 Wipe out the frying pan with some paper towel. Reheat the pan over medium heat and add the remaining oil. Fry the patties, in batches – being careful not to overcrowd the pan – until golden, about 3 minutes on each side. Drain on paper towel.

VARIATIONS

✔ Use lentils, chickpeas, borlotti beans or any bean instead of the navy beans.

✔ Add: a few anchovy fillets with the onion or leek and allow to melt; 1 tbsp grated lemon or lime zest with the veggies; 2 tsp ground cumin or curry paste after the onion or leek has softened and stir for 1 minute; or 185 g (6½ oz/1 cup) cooked quinoa, millet or brown rice with the legumes.

✔ Serve with: Tahini dressing or Hummus (page 160), Broccoli and mint pesto (page 55) or Green sauce (page 169).

CHOPPED SALAD WITH BLACK BEANS AND POMEGRANATE MOLASSES

GF DF VG V SF NF GrF

Chopped salads are popular in Middle Eastern cuisine. Chop everything up to a similar size then toss it all in a bowl together and dress. I use a fine sieve to drain and rinse my tinned beans. (Be sure any tinned food you buy proudly displays no BPAs are used in the lining. This highly toxic substance leaches into the food inside.) Of course, you can use soaked and cooked dried beans if you have the time or inclination. See Lentil salad with spiced yoghurt (page 80) for how to easily do this.

1 × 400g (14 oz) BPA-free tin black beans, drained and rinsed

½ Lebanese cucumber, diced

½ small red onion, diced

1 red capsicum, diced

1 dill pickle, diced

1 tbsp diced preserved lemon

50 g (1¾ oz/1 cup) chopped herbs (such as coriander, basil, mint or flat-leaf parsley)

2 tsp pomegranate molasses

2 tsp red wine vinegar

1 tbsp olive oil

1 tsp unrefined salt

1   In a large bowl, toss all the ingredients together. Taste and adjust the seasoning.

VARIATIONS

✓ Add 185 g (6½ oz/1 cup) cooked quinoa, brown rice, barley or Ancient grains (page 130).

✓ Use 1 tbsp grated lemon zest instead of the preserved lemon.

✓ Replace the red onion with 2 spring onions.

LUNCHBOX IDEAS

There are some gorgeous lunchboxes made from sustainable materials available these days; some with different compartments, others that stay hot or cold for up to three hours, and some with two or three layers with side clips. Lunch has come a long way from a white bread sandwich, wrapped in plastic and squeezed into a plastic lunchbox leaching toxic chemicals. Vary the amount and preparation of the ingredients below, depending on the age and preferences of the person.

VEGGIES

1 celery stalk, julienned

1 small carrot, julienned

3 sun-dried tomatoes, thinly sliced

3 cherry tomatoes, halved

⅓ cup peas or shelled broad beans, lightly steamed

½ small red capsicum, cut in half

1 Lebanese cucumber, quartered lengthways

FRUIT

1 slice of pineapple, cut into quarters

2 strawberries, halved

1 apple, quartered

1 kiwifruit, peeled and halved

1 pear, quartered

1 mandarin, peeled

1 small orange, quartered

1 banana

1 date

4 olives

PROTEIN

½ cup Marinated tofu (page 131) or Tamari tempeh sticks (page 140)

1 hard-boiled egg, left whole in the shell

1 Fantastic veggie fritter (page 28)

1 slice of Cauliflower, kale and caraway frittata (page 65)

½ cup any cooked legume, like navy beans or chickpeas

GRAINS

1 Flatbread (page 134)

3–4 brown rice or spelt crackers

1 slice of spelt sourdough

1 slice of gluten-free flatbread

IN A SEPARATE CONTAINER

2 tbsp feta

75 g (2¾ oz/⅓ cup) Hummus (page 160),
guacamole or Baba ghanoush with
pomegranate seeds (page 172)

95 g (3¼ oz/⅓ cup) yoghurt drizzled with 1 tsp
coconut nectar and sprinkled with 1 tsp hemp
seeds

90 g (3¼ oz/⅓ cup) cooked penne tossed in
Green sauce (page 169), Tahini dressing (page
160) or Broccoli and mint pesto (page 55)

SWEET TREATS

1 Cacao and coconut crackle (page 177)

1 piece of Coconut and peanut butter rough
(page 189)

1 Coconut and cacao cookie (page 156)

1 tsp each of raw honey and tahini or Chocolate
coconut spread (page 167) on ½ piece of
Flatbread (page 134) or a cracker, cut in half

1 Bliss ball (page 148)

1 Fruit-free muesli bar (page 142)

1 piece of Tahini and date fudge (page 185)

1 Super natural food bar (page 155)

1 Banana nut cupcake (page 180)

1 Choose at least one thing from each section, apart
from 'Sweet Treats', which should be limited to only
one serving. Pop them into a lunchbox with sections
or in small containers, then into a bigger lunchbox.

SANDWICHES AND WRAPS

Lunches are something many of us struggle to keep interesting, yet there are so many possibilities and combinations. Toasting the wraps or sandwiches seals them, keeping the filling securely inside.

BREAD

spelt or rye sourdough, spelt mountain bread or a gluten-free bread

PROTEIN

Tamari tempeh sticks (page 140)

Marinated tofu (page 131)

Cauliflower, kale and caraway frittata (page 65)

Seven-spiced baked beans (page 100)

Fantastic veggie fritters (page 28)

Hummus (page 160)

Quinoa breakfast patties (page 10)

tinned wild Alaskan salmon

VEGGIES

Include almost any veggie, such as carrot, eggplant, tomato, beetroot, pumpkin, mushroom, fennel, red cabbage, cucumber or sweet potato. Roast, sauté, shave or slice, using a mandoline, or grate, keeping them raw.

SPREADS

Add a spread such as mustard, Aioli (page 165), Broccoli and mint pesto (page 55), Baba ghanoush with pomegranate seeds (page 172), olive tapenade, whole-egg mayo, Tahini dressing (page 160), Hummus (page 160) or avocado.

LEAFY GREENS

Add any type of lettuce, rocket, baby or Japanese spinach leaves, mesclun or herbs.

CHEESE

Finally, include a cheese, such as bocconcini, feta, goat's cheese or labne.

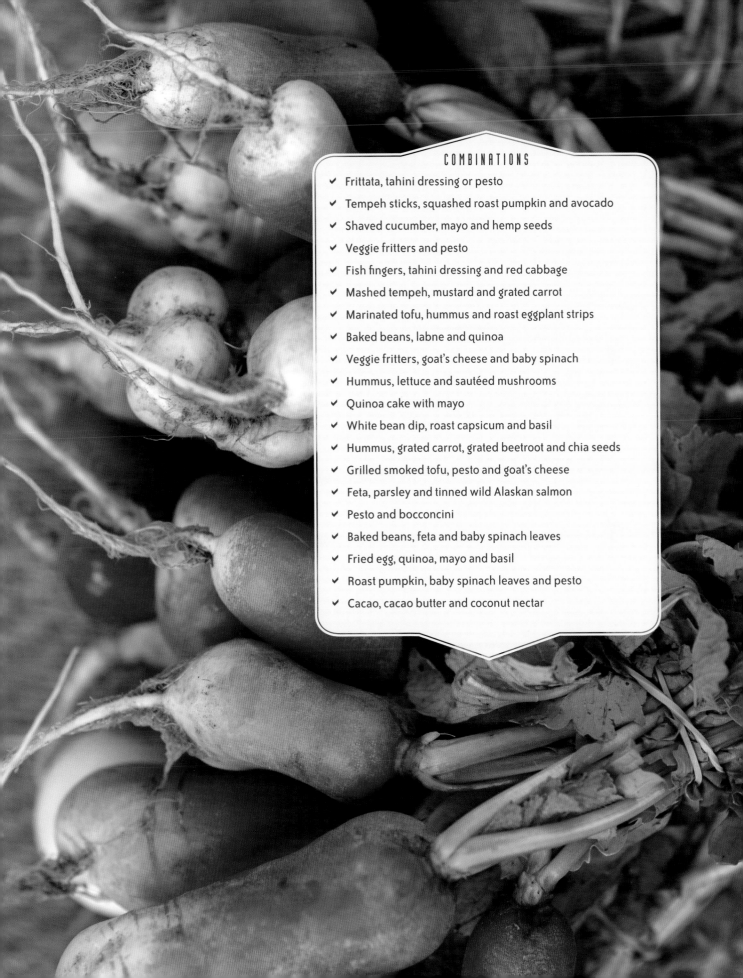

COMBINATIONS

- ✔ Frittata, tahini dressing or pesto
- ✔ Tempeh sticks, squashed roast pumpkin and avocado
- ✔ Shaved cucumber, mayo and hemp seeds
- ✔ Veggie fritters and pesto
- ✔ Fish fingers, tahini dressing and red cabbage
- ✔ Mashed tempeh, mustard and grated carrot
- ✔ Marinated tofu, hummus and roast eggplant strips
- ✔ Baked beans, labne and quinoa
- ✔ Veggie fritters, goat's cheese and baby spinach
- ✔ Hummus, lettuce and sautéed mushrooms
- ✔ Quinoa cake with mayo
- ✔ White bean dip, roast capsicum and basil
- ✔ Hummus, grated carrot, grated beetroot and chia seeds
- ✔ Grilled smoked tofu, pesto and goat's cheese
- ✔ Feta, parsley and tinned wild Alaskan salmon
- ✔ Pesto and bocconcini
- ✔ Baked beans, feta and baby spinach leaves
- ✔ Fried egg, quinoa, mayo and basil
- ✔ Roast pumpkin, baby spinach leaves and pesto
- ✔ Cacao, cacao butter and coconut nectar

JAPANESE NOODLES AND VEGGIES IN A BROTH

GF DF VG V NF GrF

You can use dried shiitake mushrooms. Just reconstitute them first in boiling water for about ten minutes, then take the stems off and slice the caps. I keep the liquid to use as stock in other dishes, or freeze it for a later time.

1 × 400 g (14 oz) packet 100% buckwheat or gluten-free kelp noodles

4 fresh shiitake mushrooms, sliced

113 g (4 oz/1 cup) bean sprouts, blanched for 1 minute, then drained

handful julienned green beans

1 carrot, julienned, blanched for 2 minutes, then drained

1 cup julienned firm tofu

2 spring onions, thinly sliced

2 tbsp wasabi

DRESSING

4 tbsp tamari

4 tbsp apple cider vinegar

2 tbsp mirin

2 tbsp sake

50 g (1¾ oz/⅓ cup) sesame seeds, ground

1 spring onion, thinly sliced

250 ml (9 fl oz/1 cup) vegetable stock

1 Cook the noodles according to the packet instructions. Buckwheat noodles are delicate as they don't contain gluten, so be careful not to overcook them (they will go gluggy and break up). Shake the noodles dry. Kelp noodles need to be soaked in water for only a few minutes, then drained.

2 For the dressing, combine the tamari, vinegar, mirin, sake, sesame seeds, spring onion and stock in a small saucepan and heat gently. Remove from the heat.

3 To serve, place the noodles in a large bowl or in individual bowls and arrange the mushrooms, bean sprouts, beans, carrot, spring onion and tofu on top. Transfer the dressing to a small jug or jugs to pour over the veggies when ready to eat. Serve the wasabi in a small dish at the table.

UDON NOODLE SALAD WITH TEMPEH AND SWEET POTATO CROUTONS

GF DF VG V NF

The Tempeh and sweet potato croutons included in this recipe are more than a fabulous substitute for the more traditional white bread variety baked in butter (or margarine). Make them fresh each time so they'll be nice and crunchy. The dressing here is lovely for any noodle dish, and with the addition of the croutons it's likely to become a favourite at your place.

1 × 200 g (7 oz) packet 100% buckwheat udon or gluten-free green tea noodles

1 tbsp arame

1 tbsp lemon juice

2 tbsp tamari

1 tbsp syrup sweetener

1 tsp mirin

1 tsp rice wine vinegar

½ cup Tempeh and sweet potato croutons (page 174)

1 sheet of nori, shredded

60 g (2¼ oz/1 cup) sunflower sprouts

1 Cook your noodles as per the packet instructions. Before you drain them, line the base of a colander with the arame, then pour the noodles over the top. This will hydrate the seaweed. Shake the excess water off the noodles. Transfer the noodles and arame to a large bowl.

2 In a small bowl, mix together the lemon juice, tamari, sweetener, mirin and vinegar and pour over the noodles.

3 Serve the noodles on individual plates or a big platter, sprinkle with the croutons, then top with the nori and sprouts.

VARIATIONS

✔ Use radish, baby daikon (white radish) or broccoli sprouts instead of the sunflower sprouts.

✔ Toss some thinly sliced Japanese spinach leaves through the noodles before tossing in the dressing.

✔ Add 1 cup steamed fresh, shelled broad beans, or peas.

BARLEY AND BEETROOT SALAD

DF VG V SF NF

This is a really pretty salad that looks wonderful on a large serving platter with some fresh flowers scattered around. If you want this as a complete meal, then add a protein, like a 400 g (14 oz) BPA-free tin of lentils or another legume, some grilled tempeh, a third of a cup of hemp seeds or nuts, like pistachios or cashews.

100 g (3½ oz/½ cup) pearl barley

375 ml (13 fl oz/1½ cups) water

1 tbsp arame

80 g (2¾ oz/½ cup) diced pumpkin, steamed

1 corn cob, steamed and kernels removed

50 g (1¾ oz/½ cup) freshly chopped herbs like mint, basil, fennel tips, dill, coriander, parsley or thyme

2 tbsp sunflower seeds, sprinkled with 1 tsp tamari and toasted

1 tsp sumac

grated zest and juice of 1 lemon

1 tsp balsamic vinegar

1 beetroot, boiled until tender, then peeled and diced

1 Put the barley in a saucepan and wash it well, then drain. Add the water and arame and place over high heat, with the lid half on. Bring to the boil, then reduce the heat to low and simmer until almost all the water has been absorbed, about 10–15 minutes. Taste. If the barley's almost cooked, remove from the heat, put the lid on and continue to cook in its own heat for another 10–20 minutes. If it's still a bit firm, add a little more water and simmer over low heat for a little longer before turning heat off and allowing to steam.

2 Once the barley's tender and cooled a little, transfer to a large bowl, add the pumpkin, corn, herbs, sunflower seeds, sumac, lemon zest and juice and vinegar and toss to combine.

3 Place in a large serving dish and scatter the beetroot over the top. Serve warm or at room temperature.

VARIATIONS

✔ Add 1 tbsp olive, macadamia or walnut oil.

✔ Include 2 tbsp each of pepitas and sesame seeds to the sunflower seeds before toasting them.

✔ For a touch of sweetness, add ½ cup dried cranberries, raisins, goji berries, chopped dates or currants.

✔ Mix in some other veggies, like steamed carrot, beans, peas or broccoli, diced celery or sliced snow peas.

✔ Use any vinegar you like.

CORN AND COCONUT PATTIES

GF DF V SF GrF

The spice paste I use here has no chilli or other forms of heat in it so these patties will suit the whole family. Of course, you may add a few bird's eye chillies if you and your family like it hot. Make triple the amount of patties and freeze in smaller portions, or keep in the fridge for at least a week.

2 corn cobs

1 tbsp coconut oil, plus extra for frying

3 eggs

3 tbsp freshly sliced, desiccated or shredded coconut

3 spring onions, white part only, thinly sliced

unrefined salt and cracked white pepper

30 g (1 oz/1 cup) coriander leaves, to serve

PASTE

3 French shallots, roughly chopped

2 garlic cloves, roughly chopped

1 tsp grated fresh ginger

3 macadamia nuts, roughly chopped

1 tsp ground coriander

1 tsp ground cumin

1 tbsp grated fresh or 1 tsp ground turmeric

1 Steam the corn then, using a sharp knife, cut off the kernels. Set aside.

2 For the paste, pound all the ingredients together using a mortar and pestle or process in a small food processor.

3 Heat the oil in a small saucepan over medium heat, stir in the spice paste and fry for 1 minute or until the paste begins to change colour and is fragrant. Transfer to a small bowl and allow to cool.

4 In a bowl, lightly whisk the eggs, then whisk in the coconut and spring onion. Next, stir in the corn kernels and the cooled spice paste and mix until thoroughly combined. Season to your liking.

5 Heat a thin layer of the extra oil in a heavy-based frying pan over medium heat. Working in batches, drop spoonfuls of the mixture into the pan and fry for 2–3 minutes on each side until golden all over.

6 Drain the patties on paper towel, then serve in stacks, topped with lots of coriander leaves.

CREAMY MUSHROOM PENNE

GF DF VG V

Truffle oil isn't so expensive considering how much you use – usually about ½ teaspoon per serve. You'll find it in grocery and specialty stores and, seriously, it's worth it. By the way, truffle oil likes basil more than it does dill, so if you are using it, then use the former as your herb of choice.

1 × 400 g (14 oz) packet gluten-free penne

2 tbsp olive oil

1 leek, pale part only, washed well, halved lengthways and thinly sliced

270 g (9½ oz/3 cups) sliced mixed mushrooms (such as Swiss, shiitake, button or oyster)

2 garlic cloves, crushed

375 ml (13 fl oz/1½ cups) almond or soy milk

1 tsp each unrefined salt and cracked black pepper

2 cups finely chopped baby spinach or silverbeet leaves

⅓ cup basil leaves or dill tips

grated zest of 1 lemon

truffle oil, to serve (optional)

1 Cook the pasta according to the packet instructions, drain, keeping a little of the cooking water, then return to the pan.

2 Heat the olive oil in a frying pan over medium heat, add the leek and sauté for 2 minutes until translucent.

3 Add the mushrooms and garlic and sauté until the mushrooms begin to soften, about 3 minutes.

4 Pour in the milk, stir and simmer for about 2 minutes until the sauce starts to thicken a little. Season with the salt and pepper.

5 Add the spinach or silverbeet, basil or dill (leave some to garnish) and zest to the pasta, stir, then pour on the sauce and gently toss to combine. Finish with the reserved dill or basil. Finish with a drizzle of truffle oil, if using.

VARIATIONS

✔ Add 2 anchovy fillets with the leek and allow to melt.

✔ Use ½ tbsp Flavoured salt (page 164) instead of unrefined salt.

✔ Try 2 large zucchini, sliced into half moons instead of the mushrooms.

✔ Grate 180 g (6½ oz) firm tofu and add with the mushrooms.

✔ Add 65 g (2½ oz/¾ cup) crumbled goat's feta to the pasta when you add the sauce.

✔ Garnish with 80 g (2¾ oz/½ cup) toasted almonds or pine nuts.

VIETNAMESE PANCAKES

GF DF V VG NF

I realise there seem to be a lot of ingredients for this recipe, and that it may look complicated, but it really is super-easy and you probably have most of the ingredients already in your kitchen. I grow my own Thai basil because I love it and I know it's sometimes tricky to find. I like to make the pancakes ahead of time and have them stacked, ready to serve separately with a platter of the sauce-drizzled veggies. It's nice to let everyone design and roll their own. The method is on the next page.

BATTER

125–160 g (4½–5¾ oz/¾–1 cup) white rice flour

1 egg

½ tsp unrefined salt

1 tsp ground turmeric

1 × 400 ml (14 fl oz) BPA-free tin coconut milk

unrefined sunflower, coconut, macadamia or avocado oil to fry

FILLING

2 carrots, grated or julienned

200 g (7 oz/2 cups) snow peas, thinly sliced on the diagonal

4 spring onions, sliced on the diagonal (save some to garnish)

1 long green chilli, thinly sliced on the diagonal

30 g (1 oz/1 cup) coriander leaves

30 g (1 oz/1 cup) Thai basil leaves

20 g (¾ oz/1 cup) mint leaves

1 cup mung bean sprouts

SAUCE

2 tbsp lime juice

1 tbsp sesame oil

1 tbsp coconut palm sugar

1 tbsp rice wine vinegar

1 tbsp tamari

1 tsp syrup sweetener (optional)

2 tsp grated fresh ginger

1 long red chilli, finely chopped

1 garlic clove, crushed

1   For the batter, combine the rice flour, egg, salt and turmeric in a large bowl. Slowly whisk in the coconut milk, avoiding lumps. Whisk in more coconut milk or water until it's the consistency of pouring cream. If the batter thickens before you are ready to use it, you may have to whisk in more liquid. Set aside.

2   To make the filling, mix together all the veggies (remembering to reserve some of the spring onion) and herbs and set aside.

3   For the sauce, combine all the ingredients in a small saucepan, place over low heat and stir until the sugar and syrup have dissolved. Adjust the seasoning and heat to your liking.

4   To make the pancakes, heat a heavy-based frying pan over medium–high heat and add a little oil. Pour in about one-quarter of the batter and swirl around to create a flat, thin crepe. Cook for about 1 minute until the underside turns golden brown, then flip and cook on the other side until it's starting to change colour – about another minute. Remove from the pan, place on a plate and keep warm under a tea towel while you make the other three pancakes.

5   To assemble, place a pancake on each serving plate and to one side pile on a quarter of the veggies, then drizzle with some sauce. Roll up the pancake, then drizzle with some more sauce and scatter on the reserved spring onion to finish.

VARIATIONS

✔ Add 350 g (12 oz/2 cups) shredded cooked chicken to the filling.

✔ Add 2 cups chopped cooked prawns to the filling.

✔ Sprinkle with 6 thinly sliced red Asian shallots that have been fried in 3 tbsp coconut oil, then drained on paper towel.

FLATBREAD PARCELS WITH MOZZARELLA AND ALMOND PESTO

V SF

You can make these an hour or so ahead of time, then pop them in the oven to brown when you're ready to serve them. They're lovely with a side of dressed green leaves.

155 g (5½ oz/1 cup) cubed Japanese pumpkin, steamed

4 pieces of Flatbread (page 134)

1 tbsp olive oil

2 large bocconcini or buffalo mozzarella balls, torn into pieces

1 tbsp white or black sesame seeds

ALMOND PESTO

80 g (2¾ oz/½ cup) toasted almonds, roughly chopped

1 garlic clove, crushed

30 g (1 oz/1 cup) basil leaves, roughly chopped

1 tsp unrefined salt

125–185 ml (4–6 fl oz/½–¾ cup) olive oil

1 Preheat your oven to 180°C (350°F/Gas 4).

2 For the pesto, blitz briefly (or pound using a mortar and pestle) the almonds, garlic, basil and salt until just combined. Now add the oil until you have a chunky but runny paste.

3 Next, put the pumpkin in a bowl and mix with the pesto. Set aside.

4 To assemble the 2 parcels, layer 1 flatbread on top of another with a scrape of olive oil between them holding them in place. Place 2 tablespoons of the pumpkin mixture in the centre of each parcel, then top with the bocconcini. Make a parcel out of the bread by bringing the corners together with a twist at the top. You may like to pierce them with a skewer or even tie them with some kitchen string to ensure they hold together.

5 Brush the outside of the parcels with a little olive oil, then sprinkle with the sesame seeds.

6 Place on a baking tray and bake for 10 minutes until starting to turn golden brown.

VARIATIONS

✓ For a dairy-free version, replace the cheese with 1 cup grated firm tofu.

✓ Instead of parcels make little cups. Quarter the bread, then press into muffin holes, brushing the flatbread with olive oil. Bake at 180°C (350°F/Gas 4) for about 5–10 minutes until golden, allow to cool, then fill with the pumpkin mixture, cheese or anything you like.

NIÇOISE SALAD

GF DF VG V NF SF GrF

A modern take on another classic dish. The sweet and lemony dressing soaks nicely into the warm sweet potato.

280 g (10 oz/2 cups) chopped sweet potato, with skin on

2 eggs, soft boiled

1 cup trimmed green beans, blanched

1 × 400 g (14 oz) BPA-free tin navy beans, drained and rinsed

½ red onion, thinly sliced

20 g (¾ oz/1 cup) flat-leaf parsley leaves

DRESSING

1 tbsp extra virgin olive oil

1 tsp white wine vinegar

grated zest and juice of 1 lemon

1 tsp raw honey

1 tsp wholegrain mustard

1 tbsp thyme leaves

1 tsp unrefined salt

½ tsp cracked white pepper

1 Steam your sweet potato until just tender, about 10 minutes, depending on the size you've cut them. Set aside.

2 Peel your eggs, cut in half and set aside.

3 For the dressing, mix all the ingredients together until emulsified.

4 In a bowl, mix together the green beans, navy beans, onion, sweet potato and parsley. Drizzle on the dressing, saving about 1 tablespoon, and toss gently.

5 To assemble, divide the salad between two serving plates, place two egg halves on each plate and drizzle over the rest of the dressing.

VARIATIONS

✓ Use 2 × 150 g (5½ oz) skinless salmon fillets instead of, or as well as, the navy beans. Cook your salmon by steaming it in a bamboo basket or on lemon slices in a covered frying pan for about 3 minutes, keeping it a little raw in the middle. Rest for a minute, then thinly slice or flake over the salad.

✓ Omit the thyme leaves and add finely chopped flat-leaf parsley to the dressing.

✓ Lay 2 anchovy fillets on top of each salad.

✓ Use dried, cooked navy beans instead of tinned, if you prefer. (See Seven-spiced baked beans on page 100 for how to prepare them.)

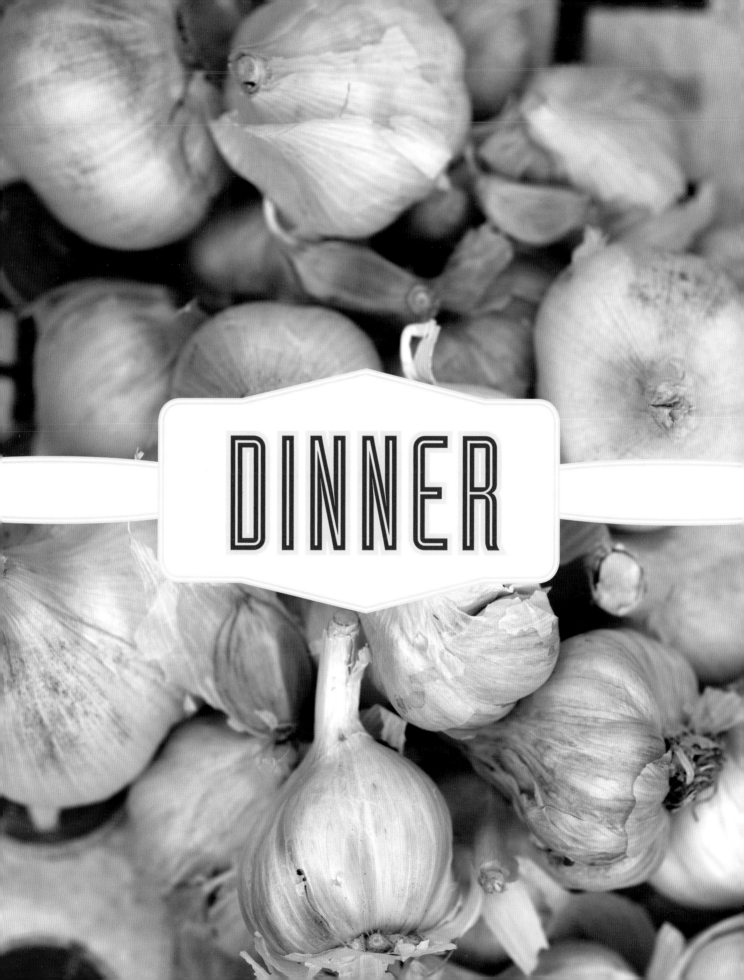

DINNER

TACOS

GF V NF

Labne is a Middle Eastern yoghurt that's been drained, so it's quite firm, like cheese. Quark is a fermented cheese that's especially good for helping to improve digestion, plus it's a good source of protein. You'll find both in health food shops and some good grocery stores. Any corn products must be Australian and organic, as corn is one of those crops that uses genetically modified technology to grow it. The method is on the following page.

1 × 300 g (10½ oz) block tempeh

1 tbsp olive or macadamia oil

1 small brown onion, diced

2 garlic cloves, crushed

2 tsp sweet or smoked paprika

2 tsp ground cumin

1 × 400 g (14 oz) BPA-free tin crushed
    tomatoes

½ tsp each unrefined salt and cracked
    black pepper, or to taste

1 × 140 g (5 oz) packet gluten-free taco
    shells

2 cups shredded cos or iceberg lettuce

130 g (4¾ oz/½ cup) labne or quark

coriander leaves and thinly sliced
    Spanish onion for garnish

GUACAMOLE

1 tomato, diced

4 basil leaves, shredded

1 Lebanese cucumber, diced

1 garlic clove, crushed

1 spring onion, finely chopped

1 tbsp lemon or lime juice

grated zest from the lemon or lime

handful of coriander leaves, roughly chopped

splash of Tabasco

½ tsp unrefined salt

1 tsp olive oil (optional)

- ✓ Add 1 tbsp coriander leaves when sautéeing the onions.

- ✓ Add 1 tbsp grated fresh turmeric or 2 tsp ground.

- ✓ For a kick, add 1 tsp cayenne pepper or dried chilli flakes with the other spices.

- ✓ Use 130 g (4¾ oz/1 cup) crumbled feta instead of the labne or the usual tasty cheese.

- ✓ Use 1 × 400 g (14 oz) BPA-free tin black beans, mashed with 1 diced small red onion, instead of the tempeh.

- ✓ Use the same amount of organic turkey, beef or lamb mince instead of the tempeh.

- ✓ Serve with a few sliced or diced dill pickles.

- ✓ To make nachos, use organic corn chips instead of taco shells, or Flatbread (page 134) cut into triangles and tossed in macadamia oil, then baked in the oven until crisp.

- ✓ For burritos, wrap the fillings in spelt flatbread or gluten-free flatbread, then warm in a steamer or oven, or toast in a sandwich press.

1 Using a food processor, quickly blitz the tempeh, keeping it a little chunky. You can also do this by hand by roughly chopping it first, then putting it in a bowl and mashing with a fork.

2 Heat the oil in a large heavy-based frying pan over medium heat. Add the onion and sauté until starting to soften, about 1 minute. Add the garlic and stir for a few seconds.

3 Next add the spices and toast for 1 minute, or until they're starting to smell fragrant.

4 Add the minced tempeh and stir to coat it in the oil and spices, then stir in the tomatoes. Allow it to simmer for about 5–10 minutes. Taste for seasoning and adjust it how you like.

5 For the guacamole, in a bowl roughly mash the ingredients together.

6 To serve the tacos, place the tempeh mixture in the pan on the table then arrange the other ingredients on a platter next to it. The labne/quark and guacamole may need to go in small bowls with a spoon on the platter. Use the labne or quark as you would sour cream. Garnish with the coriander leaves.

STEAMED SILKEN TOFU WITH SHIITAKE MUSHROOMS

GF DF VG V NF

This will likely become a regular at your place. It's quick, nourishing, yummy and uses only one pan. Use a steamer if you have one. If not, then a bamboo steamer over simmering water works well.

1 × 300 g (10½ oz) tub silken tofu, cut into 6 pieces

2 tsp shaoxing rice wine

1 tbsp tamari

1 tsp sesame oil

1 tsp rice wine vinegar

1 tbsp grated fresh ginger

4 fresh shiitake mushrooms, halved

125 ml (4 fl oz/½ cup) water

185 g (6½ oz/1 cup) cooked brown rice or quinoa or Ancient grains (page 130)

1 bunch of broccolini, trimmed and halved lengthways

1 tbsp toasted sesame seeds, to garnish

1 Place a shallow bowl in a steamer basket over a wok or saucepan of simmering water. Place the tofu, rice wine, tamari, sesame oil, vinegar, ginger, mushrooms and water as well as the cooked rice, quinoa or grains and broccolini in the bowl. Cover with a lid and steam for 3–4 minutes until the broccolini is just tender, and the grains and broth warmed through. Serve garnished with the sesame seeds.

VARIATIONS

✓ Use 1 tsp coconut or brown rice vinegar instead of the shaoxing rice wine.

✓ Add 1 tsp fish sauce with the tamari.

✓ Use 2 × 100 g (3½ oz) pieces of fish or chicken instead of the tofu. Cut in half so it cooks faster – about 6–8 minutes, respectively.

✓ Add 1 tsp grated fresh turmeric.

✓ Garnish with a handful of coriander leaves, sliced spring onion and 1 tbsp hemp seeds.

WARM FREEKEH AND GRILLED CAPSICUM SALAD

V SF NF

Freekeh is a young wheat grain popular in Middle Eastern cooking that is smoked to increase its digestibility. It's also sun-dried and thrashed around a bit. It is this 'thrashing' or rubbing process of the grains that gives this food its name, fark or 'rubbed'. When cooked, freekeh is similar to pearl barley as it too has a chewy and nutty texture. Many people with gluten intolerances seem to be able to handle this without problems. Personally I'm okay with the cracked freekeh but the whole grain is a bit of a challenge. Freekeh is becoming more widely available now, and its nutritional value acknowledged, which is wonderful, but if you can't locate it, use pearl barley, quinoa, brown rice or a mixture of them all.

1 red capsicum, halved lengthways and deseeded

½ cup freekeh, cracked or whole

375 ml (13 fl oz/1½ cups) water

1 small red onion, thinly sliced

1 garlic clove, crushed

½ tsp ground allspice

¼ tsp smoked paprika

1 tbsp each fresh or 1 tsp dried oregano and thyme

45 g (1¾ oz/¼ cup) green or black olives, halved and pitted

65 g (2½ oz/½ cup) crumbled goat's feta

2 tbsp lemon juice

3 tbsp olive oil

1 tbsp raw honey

1 tsp pomegranate molasses

unrefined salt

1   Heat the grill to high. Place the capsicum, cut side down, under the grill and cook until starting to blacken. Remove from grill, pop in a plastic bag or dish with a lid and allow to sweat for a few minutes. When cool enough to handle, peel, then discard the skin. Slice the flesh into thin strips. Set aside.

2   Meanwhile, wash the freekeh well, then place in a saucepan and cover with the water. With the lid half on, bring to the boil, then reduce the heat to low and simmer until the freekeh is tender, about 15 minutes. Take off the heat and cover completely with the lid. Leave to sit for at least 10 minutes so the freekeh keeps cooking in its own steam.

3   In a large bowl, mix together the freekeh, onion, garlic, spices, herbs, capsicum, olives and feta.

4   In a separate smaller bowl, make the dressing by whisking together the lemon juice, oil, honey, pomegranate molasses and salt.

5   Toss the dressing through the freekeh. Taste and adjust the seasoning to how you like it.

SPELT PASTA WITH BROCCOLI PESTO

V SF

This is my take on the more traditional spaghetti with pesto, which I love but can't digest very well. All that white pasta and yellow cheese just isn't my thing. Spelt pasta is much easier to digest or, if you're completely gluten-free, then use a different pasta. I've also used feta instead of the parmesan usually used. Of course leave this out if you're vegan or dairy-free. Make more and freeze it for convenience, although you will lose a little of the broccoli's bright green colour. It'll keep for three months in the freezer.

400 g (14 oz) spelt pasta (big shells will hold the pesto nicely)

1 cup Broccoli and mint pesto (opposite)

1 Bring a large saucepan of water to the boil, add the pasta and cook according to the packet instructions. Drain, keeping about 125 ml (4 fl oz/½ cup) of the cooking water in the pan.

2 Return the pasta to the pan, then add the pesto and some of the reserved cooking water, if necessary, tossing gently until combined.

VARIATIONS

- ✓ Toss 1 × 200 g (7 oz) BPA-free tin wild Alaskan salmon into the pasta with the pesto.

- ✓ Poach or bake 2 × 150 g (5½ oz) chicken breasts or fish fillets (or use leftovers). Shred or flake, then add to the pasta with the pesto.

- ✓ Add 160 g (5¾ oz/¾ cup) sun-dried or oven-baked tomatoes to the sauce.

BROCCOLI AND MINT PESTO

GF V SF GrF

Pesto is another sauce I make often, changing the ingredients depending on what I have in the fridge. It really does lend itself to any nuts, herbs, seeds and now – broccoli. Leave out the cheese for a dairy-free and vegan option.

1 small head of broccoli, cut into florets

20 g (¾ oz/1 cup) mint, roughly chopped

1–2 garlic cloves, chopped

50 g (1¾ oz/⅓ cup) chopped almonds

50 g (1¾ oz/⅓ cup) crumbled goat's feta

1 tsp unrefined salt, or to taste

1 tbsp grated lemon zest

125 ml (4 fl oz/½ cup) extra virgin olive oil

1 Steam the broccoli and garlic for a minute, or until the broccoli is just tender.

2 Using a food processor or mortar and pestle, pulse or pound the broccoli, mint, garlic, almonds, feta, salt and lemon zest to form a chunky paste. Drizzle in the olive oil and process or pound until you have your desired consistency of crunchy peanut butter.

VARIATIONS

✓ Toasting the almonds first will make the pesto yummier.

✓ Use parmesan instead of the feta.

✓ Add 1 cup chopped kale to the broccoli when steaming.

✓ Add 60 g (2¼ oz/2 cups) herbs to the blender; try coriander, basil or rocket.

✓ Any nut will work: walnuts, pistachios, macadamias, pine nuts, Brazil nuts or cashews.

✓ Use sunflower or hemp seeds instead of the almonds.

SPAGHETTI AND 'MEAT' BALLS

DF VG V NF

Australia's favourite meal just got better. I've never had anyone spot that I'd used tempeh instead of beef in this dish. Keep the tempeh a little chunky so it resembles beef and serve these balls either in a Napoli sauce with pasta or on their own as finger food. The method is on the following page.

1 × 400 g (14 oz) packet spelt spaghetti

½ cup each chopped flat-leaf parsley and basil leaves

BALLS

1 × 300 g (10½ oz) block tempeh

1 tbsp olive oil

1 white or brown onion, diced

2 celery stalks, diced

2 garlic cloves, chopped

1 carrot, grated

1 zucchini, grated

1 cup finely chopped mixed herbs (such as oregano, basil, flat-leaf parsley or chives)

2 tsp chia seeds

2 tsp brown rice flour

unrefined salt and cracked black pepper

NAPOLI SAUCE

1–2 tbsp olive oil, depending on your preference

1 medium brown onion, diced

1 garlic clove, crushed

2 × 400 g (14 oz) BPA-free tins diced tomatoes

1 tbsp tomato paste

1 bay leaf

1 tsp each unrefined salt and cracked black pepper

FRIED RICE

GF DF V NF

This is a trusty old favourite of mine that I've played around with over time. These days I use coconut oil instead of olive oil, add grated fresh turmeric and smoked tofu and more veggies, like corn and diced zucchini. I also like to cook my rice with shiitake mushrooms and a seaweed, such as arame, dulse or powdered nori. Fried rice is another dish to make in bulk and freeze in portions for up to three months. The method is on the following page.

2 tbsp coconut oil

1 onion, diced

2 garlic cloves, crushed

1 tbsp grated fresh ginger

1 tbsp grated fresh turmeric

2 tbsp chopped coriander roots and stems

2 celery stalks, diced

2 corn cobs, kernels removed

1 cup peas, thinly sliced green beans or diced zucchini

185 g (6½ oz/1 cup) diced smoked tofu

1 tbsp tamari

1 tsp sesame oil

740 g (1 lb 10 oz/4 cups) cooked organic brown rice, long or short grain

4 spring onions, sliced on the diagonal

1 long red chilli, finely chopped (optional)

50 g (1¾ oz/1 cup) chopped coriander leaves

OMELETTE

4 eggs

2 tsp mirin (optional)

½ tsp tamari (optional)

pinch of unrefined salt (optional)

2 tbsp coconut oil

- ✔ Use olive oil if you don't like coconut oil.

- ✔ Add 4 anchovy fillets with the garlic.

- ✔ Use firm tofu if you can't find smoked.

- ✔ Season with 1 tbsp fish sauce, adding it with the tamari.

- ✔ I like to add 2 cups chopped kale with the veggies or a handful of baby spinach leaves at the end when I add the omelette.

- ✔ I sometimes add the coconut pulp I have left over after making coconut milk.

- ✔ Cook 100 g (3½ oz) diced fish, green prawns or chicken with the oil, onion, garlic and spices.

1. For the omelette, whisk your eggs with the mirin, if using. You don't need to add any seasoning to the eggs but you can add a splash of tamari or a pinch of salt if you like.

2. Heat the oil in a wok or large frying pan over medium heat. Pour in the egg mixture and cook until it starts to set and puffs up. It'll curl up around the edges and start to turn a golden colour. This will take only about 30 seconds. Flip, then cook for a further 30 seconds with the heat off. Place it on a cutting board and allow to cool a little.

3. Now roll it up and slice into thin strips. Set aside.

4. Wipe the wok or pan with paper towel, add the coconut oil and melt over medium heat. Add the onion, garlic, ginger, turmeric and coriander roots and stems and sauté for 1 minute or until fragrant.

5. Toss in all the veggies and stir-fry until almost tender, about 5 minutes.

6. Next, add the tofu, tamari and sesame oil, stir, and sauté for another minute.

7. Lastly, add the rice, spring onion, chilli, if using, coriander leaves and omelette strips and stir well to combine. Serve.

CAULIFLOWER, KALE AND CARAWAY FRITTATA

GF V SF NF GrF

I really love making and eating frittatas. Everything in one dish always appeals to me, especially when I can make a few versions from the same basic recipe. Sometimes I make mini frittatas in muffin holes, add cooked quinoa to the base, then freeze them. Be sure to get organic free-range eggs to avoid any chemicals in their feed and to ensure the hens have been treated nicely.

1 small cauliflower, cut into florets

6 eggs

4 tbsp quark

4 tbsp soft goat's feta

2 tbsp dijon mustard

1 tbsp caraway seeds

unrefined salt and cracked black pepper

1 tbsp olive oil

1½ cups chopped kale

1   Preheat the oven to 180°C (350°F/Gas 4).

2   Lightly steam the cauliflower until just tender. Set aside.

3   In a large bowl, whisk the eggs, quark, feta, mustard and caraway seeds. Season with salt and pepper.

4   Heat the oil in a large ovenproof (preferably cast-iron) frying pan over medium heat, add the cauliflower and fry, without stirring, for 2 minutes until golden on one side. Turn and fry until golden on the other side. Add the kale and allow to wilt a little. Pour in the egg mixture and move the veggies around the pan with a fork so they are evenly spaced. Cook for about 5 minutes until the egg starts to set and the underside browns.

5   Transfer the pan to the oven to finish cooking, around 10–15 minutes. Remove from the oven and leave to settle for a few minutes before tucking in.

VARIATIONS

✔ Use cow's or sheep's feta if you don't like goat's feta.

✔ Substitute bocconcini for the quark, or use both.

✔ Toasting the caraway seeds first gives them a stronger flavour. Add them to the pan with the cauliflower.

POLENTA-CRUSTED TEMPEH

GF DF VG V NF

You know when you get the invite to a barbie and you're thinking, What will I take instead of rissoles or sausages? This is it. Take the sweet potato all ready to be popped on the barbie with the tempeh. This recipe can be easily doubled or tripled to feed a crowd. I have served it with Aioli (page 165).

160 g (5¾ oz/1 cup) brown rice flour

95 g (3¼ oz/½ cup) fine polenta

1 tsp sweet paprika

1 tsp cumin seeds

1 tsp ground coriander

1 tbsp curry powder

1 tsp dried thyme

½ tsp unrefined salt

250 ml (9 fl oz/1 cup) soy milk

2 tbsp dijon mustard

1 × 300 g (10½ oz) block tempeh, cut into 4 triangular pieces

2 tbsp coconut or macadamia oil (more if you want to shallow-fry it)

Herbed sweet potato chips (page 153), to serve

DRESSING

125 ml (4 fl oz/½ cup) lemon juice

2 garlic cloves, crushed

1 tsp unrefined salt

1 For the polenta crust, mix together the flour, polenta, paprika, cumin, coriander, curry powder, thyme and salt on a plate.

2 Whisk the milk and mustard in a bowl.

3 Firmly press the tempeh pieces into the polenta crumbs, coating all sides, dip into the milk mixture, then coat again in the polenta crumbs.

4 Heat the oil in a large heavy-based frying pan over medium–high heat. Or place it straight on the barbie. Add the tempeh and cook on all sides for 2 minutes or until golden. Drain on paper towel.

5 Meanwhile, for the dressing, whisk the lemon juice, garlic and salt in a small bowl. Taste and adjust the seasoning, if you like.

6 To assemble, place two overlapping triangles of tempeh on each plate with a pile of herbed sweet potato chips. Serve the dressing in little bowls on the side.

VARIATIONS

✓ Barbecue the tempeh instead of pan-frying. In this case brush a little oil on the barbecue plate first. Or bake it, turning once, at 180°C (350°F/Gas 4) for 15 minutes. Grilling is another option.

SPICY NOODLES, SMOKED TOFU AND VEGETABLES

GF DF VG V NF

This is a colourful, tasty and easy dish.

150 g (5½ oz) 100% buckwheat or gluten-free kelp noodles

1 tbsp macadamia oil

1 × 200 g (7 oz) block smoked tofu, cubed

2 garlic cloves, thinly sliced

135 g (4¾ oz/1½ cups) thinly sliced fresh shiitake mushrooms

100 g (3½ oz/1 cup) thickly sliced snow peas

1 carrot, julienned

1 spring onion, sliced

25 g (1 oz/½ cup) chopped coriander leaves

SPICY SAUCE

2 garlic cloves, crushed

1 tbsp grated fresh ginger

2 lemongrass stems, white part only, finely chopped

1 tsp dried chilli flakes

3 tbsp dry sherry

500 ml (17 fl oz/2 cups) water

3 tbsp tamari

4 tbsp brown rice syrup

- Smoked tofu is not always easy to find. Use firm tofu instead.

- You can use dried shiitake mushrooms. First soak them in boiling water for about 10 minutes or until soft. Drain, remove the stems and discard (add to your stock bag), then finely slice the caps.

- Serve with toasted sesame seeds scattered on top.

- Use 100 g (3½ oz) sliced chicken or flaked fish instead of the tofu. Poach the fish in the sauce first, and cook the chicken in a little oil before adding the garlic and veggies.

1 Cook the buckwheat noodles according to the packet instructions. Drain and immediately refresh in cold water to prevent them from becoming gooey. Soak the kelp noodles in water for a few minutes, drain well then set aside.

2 For the sauce, place all the ingredients in a small saucepan and bring to the boil. Drop the heat to low and simmer for a couple of minutes until it's warm and reduced a little. Remove from the heat and allow to cool slightly. Strain through a fine sieve then set the sauce aside.

3 Meanwhile, heat your oil in a wok or large frying pan over medium–high heat. Stir in the tofu and toss for a minute or so until it becomes lightly golden. Now add the garlic, shiitake mushrooms, snow peas and carrot and stir-fry for another minute or two until the veggies are just tender. Stir in the sauce and bring to the boil, then add the noodles and toss well. Serve immediately, topped with the spring onion and coriander.

ZUCCHINI AND COCONUT 'PASTA' WITH CASHEW CREAM CHEESE

GF DF VG V SF GrF R

Use a little tool called a spiraliser to make 'pasta' out of the carrot and cucumber. If you don't have one then you can julienne the veggies, or use mung bean pasta or quinoa noodles. This sauce is also great on just about anything that needs some creaminess.

1 tbsp any seaweed (such as dulse or nori flakes, wakame, arame or karengo fronds)

2 tbsp water

1 young coconut, halved and flesh scooped out

1 carrot, end off

1 Lebanese cucumber

grated zest and juice of 1 lime

1 cup Cashew cream cheese (page 166)

1 Soak the seaweed in the water for 5 minutes or until soft.

2 Meanwhile, finely slice the coconut flesh. I use a spiraliser I bought in Bali which lets me get the flesh straight out of the coconut in thin strips. Set aside in a bowl. Next, use the spiraliser to create twists out of the cucumber and carrot, otherwise finely julienne, using a veggie peeler or a mandoline. Add the veggies to the coconut in the bowl along with the seaweed and its soaking liquid. Lastly add the lime zest and juice, and gently toss.

3 To serve, divide the 'pasta' between two bowls and top with the cashew cream cheese.

SHEPHERD'S PIE

GF DF VG V NF GrF

Don't let the name turn you off, especially those of you who went to boarding school or who grew up on a farm in outback Australia. (Anyone born around 1970 will know what I mean.) One bite of my version and you'll be hooked. This dish may yet come back into vogue, Janella-style.

3 large potatoes, peeled and chopped

4 garlic cloves, chopped

500 ml (17 fl oz/2 cups) soy milk

1 tsp each unrefined salt and cracked white pepper

90 g (3½ oz/2 cups) chopped silverbeet

1 tbsp olive oil, plus extra to drizzle

70 g (2½ oz/½ cup) chopped leek, pale part only, washed well

1 carrot, diced

1 large celery stalk, diced

1 tbsp thyme leaves

4 tbsp white wine

375 ml (13 fl oz/1½ cups) vegetable stock

2 tsp dijon mustard

185 g (6½ oz/1 cup) diced smoked tofu

1 × 440 g (15½ oz) BP-free tin brown lentils

30 g (1 oz/1 cup) chopped flat-leaf parsley leaves

1 Heat your oven to 180°C (350°F/Gas 4).

2 Place your potato in a large saucepan, add half the garlic and cover with the milk. Season, bring just to the boil, reduce the heat and simmer until very tender. Turn off the heat, place the silverbeet on top and cover with a lid.

3 Meanwhile, heat your oil in a flameproof dish (preferably a cast-iron saucepan) over medium heat, add the leek and sauté for 2 minutes or until translucent. Add the remaining garlic, the carrot, celery and thyme and sauté for another minute. Stir in the white wine, stock and mustard and simmer, with the lid half on, until the veggies are tender. Stir in the tofu, lentils and parsley and taste. Adjust seasoning, if necessary. It should be a little wet still, not too dry.

4 Drain and reserve any milk left in the pan with the potato and silverbeet and set aside. Using a food processor (or use a masher), pulse the spuds and silverbeet, using the reserved milk to get the right consistency for mash. Adjust seasoning to how you like it.

5 Top the veggie lentil mixture with the mash, using a fork to make peaks. Drizzle the extra oil over the top and bake for about 15 minutes until turning golden brown and the veggie mixture is bubbling up.

VARIATIONS

- ✔ You can use frozen spinach instead of the silverbeet.

- ✔ Swap the spuds for sweet potato.

- ✔ Add a handful of any fresh herbs you like – chopped basil or mint, snipped chives or 1 tsp each of dried basil, mint or chives.

- ✔ Use another protein like meat, chicken or fish instead of the lentils and tofu. Add the first two with the onion, and the fish can be added once the stock and wine are simmering. It'll only be half cooked and will finish cooking in the oven.

- ✔ Use firm tofu if you can't find smoked.

- ✔ Add ½ tsp cayenne pepper for a kick.

- ✔ Add 1 tbsp grated fresh or 1 tsp ground turmeric.

- ✔ Mix 140 g (5 oz/1 cup) of frozen peas with the lentils.

AGADASHI TOFU

GF DF VG V NF

I love this dish but I hesitate before ordering it from Japanese restaurants because I know they'll be using genetically modified tofu and trans fats, such as palm oil, to fry it in. Plus where are the nori sheets from? And what about the flour? So much to think about...Instead, I make my own – and it's so much better. Look for unbleached gluten-free cornflour, and vegan dashi, which is available from health food stores.

1 × 300 g (10½ oz) block silken tofu

125–500 ml (4–17 fl oz/½–2 cups) avocado oil

cornflour, for dusting

2 tbsp finely grated daikon (white radish)

½ nori sheet, thinly sliced

2 spring onions, thinly sliced

BROTH

1 × 10 g (¼ oz) sachet of vegan dashi stock

2 tbsp tamari

1 tbsp mirin

1 tbsp grated fresh ginger

500 ml (17 fl oz/2 cups) water

1   Carefully cut the tofu into 6 even pieces and drain in a colander for about 10 minutes. You want the tofu to be as dry as possible. Pat dry with paper towel.

2   Meanwhile, make your broth. Combine all the ingredients in a small saucepan and gently simmer for a couple of minutes.

3   Using as much oil as you like, heat your oil in a large wok or frying pan. (Either fully submerge the tofu in the oil to deep-fry it, or shallow-fry it and turn once.) Generously dust the tofu in the cornflour, then shake off any excess. Gently drop the tofu into the hot oil, being careful not to overcrowd the pan. Fry until golden all over, then drain on paper towel.

4   To serve, place 3 pieces of tofu in each of two serving bowls and pour half the broth over the top. Scatter on the daikon, nori and spring onion.

BROAD BEAN AND KELP NOODLE SALAD

GF DF VG V NF

Tamarind pulp is easy to find these days, either from Asian grocery stores or in the Asian section at the supermarket. You'll find kelp noodles at health food stores, and try to use fresh broad beans. Alternatively buy frozen ones from New Zealand. Avoid any from China.

370 g (13 oz/2 cups) shelled broad beans

½ × 300 g (10½ oz) packet gluten-free kelp noodles

90 g (3¼ oz) firm tofu, julienned

1 cup fresh herbs (such as mint, coriander, Thai basil or Vietnamese mint)

DRESSING

1 tbsp each grated fresh ginger and garlic

grated zest and juice of 1 lime

2 tsp coconut palm sugar

25 g (4½ oz/½ cup) tamarind pulp

1 tsp tamari, or to taste

1 long red chilli, halved lengthways, deseeded and thinly sliced (optional)

1 Blanch the broad beans in simmering water, refresh under cold water, peel and discard the skins. Put the beans in a salad bowl.

2 Pour boiling water over the noodles and let soak for a few minutes.

3 To make the dressing, in a small bowl mix the ginger, garlic, lime zest and juice, sugar, tamarind pulp, tamari and chilli, if using.

4 Drain the noodles and add these with the tofu and herbs to the broad beans, then gently mix in the dressing and serve.

VARIATIONS

✔ Use peas instead of broad beans. Frozen peas are fine: pour boiling water over them, let them sit for a minute, then drain.

✔ Cut the tofu into 1-cm (½-in) pieces and mix with 1 tbsp tamari and 1 tsp sesame oil, then either fry in coconut oil or bake at 180°C (350°F/Gas 4) for 10–15 minutes until golden.

✔ Instead of the kelp noodles, use 3 small bundles of soaked and drained glass noodles.

✔ Add any leftover veggies, like roasted or steamed pumpkin, beans, carrots or capsicum.

✔ Use 100–200 g (3½–7 oz) cooked fish, prawns or chicken, shredded, instead of, or as well as, the tofu.

CRISPY-FRIED TEMPEH WITH NOODLES

GF DF VG V NF GrF

Palm sugar and kecap manis are used extensively in Asian cooking but neither is an ingredient we want to be using anymore. Acres of rainforest are continually being destroyed to make way for massive palm crops as our demand for palm oil and its products increases. This unsustainable and damaging practice is rendering orangutans and the Sumatran tiger all but extinct. The coconut palm tree is a different plant that is not destroying the planet the way palm plantations are. Mix coconut palm sugar with tamari for an alternative to kecap manis, and use coconut oil instead of palm oil.

1 × 200 g (7 oz) packet mung bean noodles

4 tbsp macadamia or coconut oil, plus extra

1 × 300 g (10½ oz) block tempeh, cut into 3-cm (1¼-in) pieces

6 red Asian shallots, sliced

4 garlic cloves, sliced

1 tbsp grated fresh ginger

2 tbsp tamari

1 tbsp coconut palm sugar

handful of coriander leaves

1 Cook the noodles according to the packet instructions, drain and set aside.

2 Heat 2 tbsp of the oil in a heavy-based frying pan over high heat. Add the tempeh and cook for about 2 minutes on each side until golden brown all over. Remove from the pan and drain on paper towel.

3 Wipe out the pan, add the rest of the oil and fry the shallot, garlic and ginger over medium heat for 5 minutes or until just starting to change colour.

4 Add the tamari and sugar and stir until the sugar has melted.

5 Toss in the tempeh and stir-fry until the sauce is reduced and coats the tempeh. You may need to add a little water if the sauce gets too thick.

6 Toss in your noodles and finish with lots of coriander leaves.

VARIATION

✔ Add 1 cup of chopped broccolini, snow peas or squash to the onion and garlic mixture after they've softened.

PAELLA

GF DF VG V SF NF

I'm often asked to make this for family and friends' birthdays – by special request. When you're ready to eat, pop the pan in the centre of the table with a couple of spoons and let the rest happen, naturally.

2 tbsp olive oil

1 small red onion, diced

1 small red capsicum, thinly sliced

1 small yellow capsicum, thinly sliced

2 garlic cloves, chopped

2 bay leaves

1 tsp smoked paprika

1 tbsp grated fresh or 1 tsp ground turmeric

220 g (7¾ oz/1 cup) organic brown rice, short grain

125 ml (4 fl oz/½ cup) sherry

700 ml (24 fl oz) vegetable stock

6 tomatoes, chopped, or 1 × 400 g (14 oz) BPA-free tin diced tomatoes

1 tsp saffron threads

1–2 tsp unrefined salt

1 cup fresh or frozen peas

15 g (½ oz/½ cup) finely chopped flat-leaf parsley

1 lemon or lime, quartered, to serve

1 In a large paella pan or heavy-based frying pan, heat your oil over medium heat, add your onion and fry for 2 minutes or until softened and just starting to change colour. Stir in the capsicums and sauté until starting to soften and colour a little, about 5 minutes. Add the garlic and sauté for another minute, then add your bay leaves and spices and stir until fragrant and starting to stick to the bottom of the pan.

2 Tip your rice into the pan and stir well to coat with the spices, then add the sherry, stock, tomatoes, saffron and salt. Boil gently for a few minutes, reduce the heat to low and simmer for about 20 minutes until the liquid has been absorbed. Don't stir or cover the rice as this will make it gluggy.

3 If using frozen peas, add them to the pan. If fresh, steam them in some boiling water until just tender and then place on top of the rice.

4 Take your pan off the heat and cover with a lid, allowing it to rest for about 10 minutes. Scatter on the parsley and serve with the lemon or lime wedges.

VARIATIONS

✔ Add 4 anchovy fillets or 200 g (7 oz) sliced chicken thigh fillet with the garlic.

✔ For a seafood paella, about 5 minutes before the rice is cooked, top the paella with 100 g (3½ oz) white fish, cut into chunks, 8 peeled and deveined green prawns with tails intact and 1 cup calamari strips that have been tossed in olive oil and a little salt. Put the lid on, turn the heat off when the rice is ready and let it sit for a few minutes before serving.

LENTIL SALAD WITH SPICED YOGHURT

GF V SF NF GrF

If you're using dried lentils, to increase their digestibilty cover them in water and soak for 30–60 minutes, then drain. Cook them in plenty of clean water with a good pinch of any seaweed such as arame or powdered nori or dulse. I often skip the soaking for the smaller and split lentils. If using tinned lentils, be sure the lining is BPA-free.

210 g (7½ oz/1 cup) dried puy or brown lentils, or 1 × 400 g (14 oz) BPA-free tin drained and rinsed brown lentils

390 g (13¾ oz/1½ cups) Greek yoghurt

2 tsp olive oil

1 tsp ground cumin

1 tsp ground coriander

grated zest and juice of 1 lemon

1 tsp each unrefined salt and cracked black pepper, or to taste

½ cup sultanas, currants, goji berries or cranberries

1 cup chopped mixed herbs (such as mint, coriander, dill or flat-leaf parsley)

45 g (1¾ oz/1 cup) baby spinach or rocket leaves

½ red onion, thinly sliced

1 In a small bowl, mix together the yoghurt, oil, spices, lemon zest and juice and seasoning. In a large bowl, toss everything else together and season a little. Stir in the yoghurt mixture and serve.

VARIATIONS

- ✔ To make a Mediterranean version, swap the spices for the same amount of dried thyme, oregano and basil.

- ✔ For a dairy-free salad, leave out the yoghurt and instead add 2 diced tomatoes.

- ✔ Add other veggies, like 1 cup grated carrot and/or corn kernels, cauliflower or asparagus, even baked veggies.

- ✔ Toss in ½ cup toasted nuts (pine nuts, almonds, walnuts, macadamias), the larger ones roughly chopped.

- ✔ Finish with a sprinkle of sumac.

TANDOORI TOFU

GF DF VG V NF GrF

If you have a tajine, a clay pot traditionally used for slowly cooked dishes in many cultures, place all the ingredients in this and let it simmer away for an hour. Below is a basic recipe, but feel free to add lots of veggies, nuts, dried fruit and herbs. Double the recipe if you do this. It's also a perfect recipe for a slow cooker.

½ tsp fennel seeds

½ tsp cardamom seeds

2 tsp coriander seeds

1 tsp cumin seeds

1 tbsp paprika, sweet or hot

1 tbsp grated fresh turmeric or
   1 tsp ground turmeric

pinch of cayenne pepper

pinch of white pepper

¼ onion, finely diced

1 garlic clove, chopped

185 ml (6 fl oz/¾ cup) water

70 g (2½ oz) silken tofu

1 tsp grated lime zest

juice of 1 lime

1 × 300 g (10½ oz) block firm tofu, cut
   into large pieces

30 g (1 oz/1 cup) coriander leaves

1 In a small saucepan, lightly toast the fennel, cardamom, coriander and cumin seeds over medium heat until fragrant, about 2 minutes, and shake the pan a few times to prevent burning the spices. Pour into a mortar and pound with a pestle until finely ground.

2 Transfer the ground spices to a blender, add the paprika, turmeric, peppers, onion, garlic, water, silken tofu and lime zest and juice and process until smooth.

3 Put the firm tofu in a deep ovenproof dish and cover with the marinade. Let it marinate for at least 30 minutes, or even overnight before baking, covered at 180°C (350°F/Gas 4) for 20 minutes.

4 Serve with Ancient grains (page 130) and garnish with the coriander leaves.

VARIATIONS

✔ If you'd like to barbecue the tofu, then drain the marinade off and use it to baste the tofu during the cooking. Brush the barbecue plate with a little oil first. Cook until the tofu changes colour, turning on all sides and basting as you go.

✔ You can use 400 g (14 oz) firm fish fillets or a whole fish instead of the tofu, or 300 g (10½ oz) sliced chicken fillets or whole breasts.

✔ Use already ground spices instead of toasting and pounding the seeds yourself.

✔ Use the same quantity of quark or yoghurt instead of the silken tofu.

BURGERS

DF V SF NF

Serve these very good patties between the burger buns of your choice. I have suggested spelt sourdough buns but if you can't find any, serve the burgers with Herbed sweet potato chips (page 153) or Potato salad with broccoli and mint pesto (page 106). Toasting, then grinding, the whole spices instead of using the already ground ones is well worth the effort as the difference in taste is huge. To grind, use a mortar and pestle or a spice grinder.

2 large potatoes, diced, or 280 g (10 oz/2 cups) diced sweet potato

1 cup chopped kale or baby or Japanese spinach leaves

2 cups fresh broad beans, or shelled peas

2 garlic cloves, chopped

1 tsp ground cumin

1 tsp ground coriander

1 tbsp grated fresh turmeric or ½ tsp ground turmeric

1 tsp ground fennel

1½ tsp unrefined salt, or to taste

15 g (½ oz/½ cup) coriander leaves, chopped

55 g (2 oz/⅓ cup) brown rice flour or coconut flour

1 egg

2 tbsp macadamia or avocado oil for frying

4 spelt sourdough buns

4 heaped tbsp Hummus (page 160), Tahini dressing (page 160), Green sauce (page 169) or Aioli (page 165)

4 lettuce leaves of any type

1 avocado, sliced

1. Place the potato or sweet potato in a steamer over a saucepan of simmering water, cover and steam for about 10 minutes until nearly soft. Remove from the heat and drop the kale or spinach on top and allow to wilt a little. Drain if there is any liquid, then put in a large bowl.

2. Add the broad beans or peas, garlic, spices and salt. Roughly mash the mixture with a potato masher or pulse in a food processor.

3. Add the coriander leaves and flour, then mix in the egg and mash or pulse again. The mixture should be sticking together now. Shape into 4 patties, each large enough to fit a burger bun.

4. Heat the oil in a large frying pan over medium heat, add the patties and fry for a couple of minutes on each side until golden brown.

5. Spread a thick layer of hummus, tahini dressing, green sauce or aioli on each bun, top with a patty and some lettuce and avocado and serve.

VARIATIONS

✔ To make a vegan patty, use 2 tbsp flaxseed meal or chia seeds instead of the egg.

✔ Use dried chickpeas that you've soaked in water overnight instead of the broad beans or peas. In this case you will need to process the mixture, not mash it. And leave out the egg.

SOUPS, STEWS & CASSEROLES

RAW CARROT AND COCONUT SOUP

GF DF VG V SF NF GrF R

I first had a version of this soup in Bali at a health retreat. It was love at first slurp. This is my take on it. For a faster preparation time, you can buy the carrot juice but just make sure it's cold-pressed or at least contains no additives.

750 ml (26 fl oz/3 cups) fresh carrot juice

1 young coconut, flesh removed

1 avocado

grated zest and juice of 1 lime

1 tsp unrefined salt

1 Combine everything in your blender and blitz until smooth. Chill.

VARIATIONS

✓ Add 1 tsp grated fresh ginger and/or 1 tbsp grated fresh turmeric.

✓ For a hit of protein, fibre and healthy omega oils, add 1 tbsp each of hemp and chia seeds.

✓ Finish with a drizzle of hemp, walnut, chia, coconut or flaxseed oil.

✓ For a morning smoothie, add a banana.

CORN CHOWDER

GF DF VG V SF NF

This modern take on a classic dish is just so creamy and luscious that no one will ever know it has no cream, butter or cow's milk.

2 tbsp olive oil

1 small onion, finely chopped

1 leek, pale part only, washed well, halved lengthways and thinly sliced

2 celery stalks, thinly sliced

2 garlic cloves, crushed

3 corn cobs, kernels removed

3 small potatoes, peeled and diced

1 tbsp fresh or 1 tsp dried thyme

1 bay leaf

500 ml (17 fl oz/2 cups) vegetable stock

250 ml (9 fl oz/1 cup) dairy-free milk

1 tsp unrefined salt

¼ cup chopped flat-leaf parsley or finely snipped chives

½ tsp cayenne pepper or smoked paprika

1   Heat the oil in a large saucepan over medium heat, add the onion, leek and celery and sauté until translucent, about 5 minutes.

2   Stir in the garlic, corn, spuds, thyme and bay leaf and fry for 2 more minutes until the veggies are coated in the oil and starting to soften. Add the stock, milk and salt and bring to the boil. Reduce the heat to low and simmer for about 10 minutes until the potato is tender. Discard the bay leaf.

3   Allow the soup to cool slightly, remove half and reserve, then purée the rest. Pour the reserved soup back into the pan and simmer for 3 minutes or so until warmed through. Taste and season as needed.

4   To serve, sprinkle with the parsley or chives and cayenne pepper or smoked paprika.

VARIATIONS

✓ Use fish stock instead of vegetable stock.

✓ For a clam chowder, combine 500 g (1 lb 2 oz) clams and 250 ml (9 fl oz/1 cup) wine in a large saucepan and cook, shaking the pan a few times, until the clams open. Discard any that don't open. Remove the clams from their shells and add to the pan with the cooking liquid before you blend the soup.

PHOENICIAN CASSEROLE

GF DF VG V SF NF GrF

The seven-spice seasoning used here is one of those spice mixes that lends itself to so many dishes that you might like to make a lot and want it on hand at all times. Try it on your roast veggies, in lentil or veggie soups or even with Hummus (page 160).

2 tbsp olive oil, plus extra to drizzle

1 onion, chopped

4 garlic cloves, chopped

1 swede, cut into cubes

1 parsnip, cut into cubes

2 carrots, roughly chopped

1 eggplant, cut into cubes

1 zucchini, chopped

2 tomatoes, chopped

2 cups button mushrooms

750 ml–1 litre (26–35 fl oz/3–4 cups) vegetable stock

½ tsp each ground cinnamon, paprika (hot or smoked), cracked black pepper and unrefined salt

1 tsp Seven-spice seasoning (page 100)

handful of chopped flat-leaf parsley (optional)

1 Heat the oil in a large heavy-based saucepan over low heat, then add the onion and cook, stirring occasionally, until caramelised and golden, about 10–15 minutes. Stir in the garlic and cook for another minute, then add the veggies and stir again.

2 Cover the pan with a lid and cook the veggies for a few minutes. Increase the heat to high and add the stock, spices and seasoning. Bring to the boil, drop the heat to low and simmer uncovered for around 20 minutes until the veggies are soft and the stock has reduced a little. You may need to add more water if the casserole gets too dry and starts to stick to the base of the pan. Serve drizzled with a little more olive oil and garnish with the parsley, if you like.

VARIATION

✔ Serve with brown rice and/or quinoa and a dollop of plain yoghurt or quark.

DJUDRA

GF DF VG V SF NF

This was comfort food to me growing up. Actually it still is. It's a Lebanese staple. Mum would make this on a Sunday night (but using white rice) and we were allowed to eat it in front of the TV. Heaven! The grandkids are now enjoying this nurturing dish, and tradition – but with brown rice. We never soaked the lentils first (and still don't) but you can if you want to help their digestibility.

4 tbsp olive oil

2 brown onions, thinly sliced

210 g (7½ oz/1 cup) dried puy or tiny blue-green or brown lentils

110 g (4 oz/½ cup) brown rice, short grain

750 ml (26 fl oz/3 cups) water

½ tsp Seven-spice seasoning (page 100) (optional)

2 tsp unrefined salt

1 Heat the oil in a heavy-based saucepan over medium heat, add the onion and sauté, stirring occasionally, until golden, around 10 minutes. Take half out and set aside.

2 Add the lentils and rice to the pan with the remaining onion and stir to coat. Add the water, bring to the boil, then drop the heat to low and simmer for about 20 minutes, until the lentils and rice are soft. It tends to stick to the bottom so keep the temperature low. Stir in the reserved caramelised onion, the seven-spice seasoning and salt. Serve.

VARIATIONS

✔ Serve with a dollop of labne or plain yoghurt.

✔ You can leave out the seven-spice seasoning.

✔ For a faster Djudra, use split red or yellow lentils instead of the whole ones.

TURMERIC AND RED LENTIL SOUP

GF DF VG V SF NF GrF

If you don't have cumin seeds or turmeric close by, you can always use a packaged curry paste. Naturally, read the label to ensure it contains nothing but spices, and definitely no palm oil or sugar.

500 ml (17 fl oz/2 cups) vegetable stock

375 g (13 oz/1½ cups) chopped pumpkin

2 carrots, chopped

145 g (5½ oz/⅔ cup) split red lentils

2 garlic cloves, chopped

1 tbsp cumin seeds, toasted

1 tbsp grated fresh turmeric or 1 tsp ground turmeric

1 leek, pale part only, washed well, halved lengthways and chopped

1 × 400 ml (14 fl oz) BPA-free tin coconut milk

unrefined salt

2 tbsp finely chopped coriander or flat-leaf parsley leaves

1 Place everything apart from the salt and coriander or parsley in a large saucepan and bring to the boil. Drop the heat to low and simmer, with the lid half on, until the lentils are soft, around 15–20 minutes. You may need to add a little water if it's too thick.

2 Using a hand-held blender, blitz the soup a little, leaving it a bit chunky. Season to taste and garnish with the coriander or parsley.

VARIATIONS

✔ Use a pressure cooker instead of a saucepan. It'll take about 10 minutes to cook.

✔ Add 2 chopped tomatoes.

✔ 1 tsp cayenne pepper will give it some heat.

✔ Stir in 2 tbsp plain yoghurt or quark at the end.

✔ For a Middle Eastern-flavoured soup, use 2 tsp Seven-spice seasoning (page 100) instead of, or as well as, the cumin seeds.

✔ Use an additive-free curry paste instead of the cumin seeds and turmeric.

✔ Add 2 tsp grated fresh ginger and 2 tbsp chopped coriander stems and leaves to the pan with the turmeric.

CREAMY CAULIFLOWER AND LEEK SOUP

GF DF VG V NF GrF

A smooth, soft soup that is just as happy being made with almost any veggie instead of the cauliflower – potato, sweet potato, beetroot, kohlrabi, broccoli or pumpkin.

1–2 tbsp olive oil

1 leek, pale part only, washed well, halved lengthways and diced

1–2 garlic cloves, chopped

1 tbsp thyme, basil or sage leaves

1 small cauliflower, chopped into florets

500 ml (17 fl oz/2 cups) vegetable stock

1 × 300 g (10½ oz) block silken tofu

1 handful of chopped coriander or basil or snipped chives, to garnish

1 Heat your oil in a large saucepan over medium heat. Add the leek and sauté for 5 minutes until translucent. Add the garlic, herb of your choice and cauliflower and stir to coat in the oil. Pour in the stock and bring to the boil. Reduce the heat to low and simmer for about 10 minutes until the cauliflower is soft. You may need to add some water if it gets too thick.

2 Add the tofu to the soup and blend until smooth. Taste and adjust seasoning, if necessary. Garnish with the herb of your choice and serve.

VARIATIONS

✓ Use 1 onion instead of the leek.

✓ Add 1 tsp ground cumin or smoked paprika, or both with the leek or onion.

✓ Double the amount of stock and add ½ cup brown rice.

✓ For a creamier soup (not dairy-free), use half stock and half milk and leave out the tofu.

✓ Serve drizzled with ½ tsp truffle, pumpkin or walnut oil.

✓ Serve with toasted pepitas or raw hemp seeds.

✓ Garnish with a dollop of quark, a nut butter or pesto.

✓ Sprinkle with a pinch of cayenne pepper or smoked paprika.

PUMPKIN AND RICE SOUP

GF DF VG V SF NF

If you have a high-powered blender like a Vitamix, there's no need to peel or deseed the pumpkin. If you don't have one, peel the pumpkin and roast the seeds in the oven (or toast in a pan) with olive oil and a little salt. Use these instead of the pepitas as garnish. This is a lovely soup for older babies and toddlers if you omit the garnish.

450 g (1 lb/3 cups) roughly chopped Japanese or butternut pumpkin

1 onion, roughly chopped

1 litre (35 fl oz/4 cups) vegetable stock

185 g (6½ oz/1 cup) cooked brown rice

unrefined salt and cracked white pepper

pepitas, toasted, to garnish

2 tbsp finely chopped flat-leaf parsley, to garnish

1 Place the veggies and half the stock in a saucepan and simmer for about 10–15 minutes until the veggies are soft. Then stir in the brown rice and blend until smooth.

2 Pour the soup back into the pot and add the rest of the stock to get your desired consistency – not too thick and not too thin. Season as you like, and garnish with the pepitas and parsley.

VARIATIONS

✓ Stir through 1 tbsp miso paste before serving.

✓ Serve with a dollop of quark or plain yoghurt.

✓ Add a spice like ground cumin, turmeric, sweet paprika, curry powder or saffron.

✓ Almost any herb like sage, oregano or basil will be nice as a garnish, or add 1 tbsp of the fresh herb to the soup from the start.

DHAL

GF V NF GrF

I have a recipe for dhal in Eating for the Seasons *and I know lots of you love it. Here I've adjusted it slightly to make it even yummier. I now use coconut oil and I've added seaweed and more veggies.*

1 tbsp coconut oil

1 onion, chopped

2 tbsp chopped coriander roots and stems

2 garlic cloves, crushed

2 tsp grated fresh ginger

1 tbsp grated fresh turmeric or 1 tsp ground turmeric

2 tsp ground cumin

2 tsp garam masala

2 celery stalks, diced

1 zucchini, diced

1 large carrot, diced

225 g (8 oz/1 cup) mung dal (split yellow lentils)

500–750 ml (17–26 fl oz/2–3 cups) vegetable stock

2 tsp powdered nori or dulse flakes

1 kaffir lime leaf

1 tsp tamari, or to taste

1 tsp sesame oil

1 handful of chopped leafy greens (such as sliced Japanese or baby spinach or kale)

dollop of plain or coconut yoghurt or quark, to serve

15 g (½ oz/½ cup) coriander leaves

1   Heat the oil in a large saucepan over medium heat, then add the onion, coriander, garlic, ginger, turmeric, cumin and garam masala and sauté for 1 minute or until fragrant and starting to stick a little to the bottom of the pan. Add the veggies and mung dal and stir to coat, then pour in the stock, nori or dulse, lime leaf, tamari and sesame oil. Bring to the boil, reduce the heat to low and simmer for about 20 minutes until the veggies and lentils are soft. It'll look a bit like mushy peas. You may need to add a little water if it gets too thick and starts sticking to the bottom of the pan.

2   Before serving, turn off the heat, stir in the leafy greens and allow to wilt. Adjust the seasoning to how you like it, and serve with the yoghurt or quark and coriander leaves.

VARIATIONS

✓ Add 1 cup chopped (skin on) pumpkin or sweet potato and/or cauliflower florets with the other veggies.

✓ Pour in 250 ml (9 fl oz/1 cup) coconut milk with the stock.

✓ Serve with a sprinkle of hemp seeds.

✓ For a hot dhal, add 1 tsp cayenne pepper or dried chilli flakes with the other spices.

MINESTRONE

GF V SF

In France and Italy it's traditional to serve this rightly infamous soup with a dollop of pesto. If you don't want to peel and deseed the tomato, add half a 400 g (14 oz) BPA-free tin of diced tomatoes with the stock. This is a really good minestrone.

2 tbsp olive oil

1 leek, pale part only, washed well. halved lengthways and diced

1 large carrot, diced

2 celery stalks, diced

1 small bunch of cavolo nero or kale, roughly chopped

1 potato, diced

1 large zucchini, diced

80g (2¾ oz/½ cup) fresh or frozen peas

95 g (3¼ oz/½ cup) shelled broad beans (thawed frozen ones are fine)

1 large tomato, peeled, deseeded and diced

1–1.5 litres (35–52 fl oz/4–6 cups) vegetable stock

45 g (1¾ oz/½ cup) brown rice pasta shells or 185 g (6½ oz/1 cup) cooked brown rice

1 cup cooked borlotti beans or chickpeas

unrefined salt, to taste

½ cup Broccoli and mint pesto (page 55)

1 Heat the oil in a large saucepan over medium heat, then add the leek and cook slowly for a few minutes until softened. Try not to colour the leek too much. Stir in the carrot, celery, cavolo nero or kale, potato and zucchini, one at a time in the order I have listed them, and cook each one briefly before adding the next. (You're starting with the veggies that take longer to cook, allowing each one to release its juices.) Add the peas, broad beans and tomato and stir again.

2 Pour the stock into the pan, and bring to the boil. Drop the heat and simmer for about 20 minutes until all the veggies are almost soft. Then add the pasta and cook until al dente. Lastly stir in the legumes and heat through. If using the cooked brown rice instead of the pasta, simply stir it in with the legumes just before serving.

3 Once the pasta is cooked, taste for seasoning and serve with a dollop of pesto on top.

VARIATION

✓ Use one brown onion, diced, instead of the leek.

MILLET AND MISO VEGETABLE SOUP

GF DF VG V NF

This is a really lovely, super-quick soup to eat at any age: from 1 to 100. Millet has been shown to reduce an overgrowth of Candida and the studies being done on its role in cancer prevention are exciting. Blend this soup for babies and toddlers, and feel free to add any other veggies you have.

500 ml (17 fl oz/2 cups) vegetable stock

52 g (2 oz/¼ cup) millet

250 ml (9 fl oz/1 cup) miso (any type)

2 cups finely chopped veggies (such as Japanese spinach leaves, zucchini, bok choy, snow peas or carrots)

1 Bring the stock to a simmer over medium heat in a saucepan.

2 Wash the millet, then add it to the pan and simmer for 10 minutes.

3 Add the miso to the pan, stirring to dissolve, then add the veggies. Turn off the heat and put the lid on to let the veggies steam slightly before serving. This will take about 5 minutes.

VARIATIONS

✓ Add:

  2 tsp grated fresh ginger with the stock.

  1 tsp any seaweed with the stock.

✓ If you like it a bit saltier, add a splash of tamari.

✓ Finish with a few drops of sesame oil.

✓ Top with finely chopped spring onions.

CORN, TAPIOCA AND PUMPKIN SOUP

GF DF VG V SF NF

Tapioca and cassava are often confused. Tapioca is the starch extracted from the cassava plant. It comes in granules, flakes and powders, although it's most commonly available in the form of little round balls. Tapioca has traditionally been used as a thickening agent in pies and puddings in many cultures, from Brazil to Vietnam. Tapioca is gluten-free so we are seeing it more and more these days in breads and crackers.

875 ml (30 fl oz/3½ cups) water

1 cup peeled and chopped swede or kohlrabi

150 g (5½ oz/1 cup) chopped butternut pumpkin

2 tbsp brown rice

2 lemongrass stems, white part only, finely chopped

1 corn cob, kernels removed

1 tsp tapioca starch mixed with 2 tbsp water

10 sweet or Thai basil leaves

45 g (1¾ oz/1 cup) baby spinach leaves

1 tsp unrefined salt

1 In a large saucepan, bring the water to the boil, add the veggies and cook until they're soft – about 10 minutes.

2 Now add the rice to the veggies with the lemongrass and corn. Cook for another 10 minutes, stirring continuously, until the soup has thickened. You may need to add a little more water.

3 Next whisk in the tapioca slurry. Now add the basil, spinach and salt, then blend until semi-smooth. Adjust seasoning to how you like and serve.

VARIATION
✔ Use millet or quinoa instead of the rice.

RAW SWEET CHILLI BASIL SOUP

GF DF VG V SF NF R

You've got to love a dish like this. Everything in the blender, blitz, serve, then wonder at how incredibly generous nature is to provide everything we need.

½ avocado

½ zucchini, chopped

15 g (½ oz/½ cup) basil leaves

45 g (1¾ oz/1 cup) chopped baby spinach leaves or kale

500 ml (17 fl oz/2 cups) orange juice

1 garlic clove, crushed

2 tsp rice syrup

½ tsp cayenne pepper

1 tsp unrefined salt

2-cm (¾-in) piece of fresh ginger, grated

1   Place everything in your blender and blitz until smooth. Adjust seasoning to how you like it. Serve.

MOROCCAN PUMPKIN AND CHICKPEA CASSEROLE

GF DF VG V SF NF GrF

An easy, nourishing and warming casserole for the cooler months, and a great one for the slow cooker. Why not freeze containers half full of this for lunches, with Ancient grains (page 130) taking up the other half?

1 white onion, sliced

2 tbsp olive oil

2 garlic cloves, chopped

2 tsp curry powder

1 carrot, cut into half moons

600 g (1 lb 5 oz/4 cups) cubed butternut pumpkin

400 g (14 oz/2 cups) chopped tomatoes

240 g (8½ oz/1½ cups) pitted dates, roughly chopped

1 cup toasted nuts (such as almonds, pistachios or cashews), roughly chopped

1 tbsp preserved lemon, thinly sliced

500 ml (17 fl oz/2 cups) vegetable stock

2 tbsp tomato paste

1 tbsp coconut palm sugar or panela (optional)

1 cinnamon stick

3 cups quartered button mushrooms

1 × 400 g (14 oz) BPA-free tin chickpeas, drained and rinsed

unrefined salt and cracked black pepper

2 tbsp chopped herbs (such as basil, coriander or mint), to garnish

1 In a large saucepan over medium heat, sauté the onion in the olive oil for a few minutes until soft and golden, then stir in the garlic. Add the curry powder and cook, stirring, for a minute or two over medium–high heat until fragrant. Toss in the carrot and pumpkin and stir to coat the veggies in the spices.

2 Now add the tomatoes, dates, nuts, lemon, stock, tomato paste, sugar (if using) and cinnamon stick and bring to the boil, then reduce to a simmer and half cover the pot with a lid. Simmer for about 30 minutes until the pumpkin is just tender. Stir in the mushrooms and chickpeas and simmer for another 10 minutes until the mushrooms are soft.

3 Season to taste and serve garnished with the herbs.

VARIATIONS

✓ Add 1 tbsp grated fresh turmeric, or 1 tsp ground turmeric with the curry powder.

✓ Use pretty much any veggie or legume you have on hand.

✓ You can use 1 × 400 g (14 oz) BPA-free tin diced tomatoes instead of the chopped tomatoes or leave them out altogether.

✓ Serve with a dollop of quark or plain yoghurt.

✓ Add 1 tsp saffron threads with the stock.

SEVEN-SPICED BAKED BEANS

GF DF VG V SF NF GrF

You can use tinned beans to shorten the preparation and cooking time, while adding the flaxseed meal – to thicken and add another texture – is not essential. Flaxseed meal can thicken almost any dish. You'll just lose the omega oils during the cooking, as they don't like to be heated.

To cook dried beans, cover them with double their weight in water and add 2 tablespoons (low-allergy) bicarbonate of soda. The next day drain them, then place in a large saucepan with plenty of clean water. Bring to the boil, reduce the heat to low and simmer for at least 30 minutes until they are tender but not mooshy. If they are old beans they may seem to take forever to soften so you might need to add some more water to the pan. Large beans will obviously take longer than the smaller ones. Don't add any salt to the pan or they will never soften. When they are soft drain and use how you like.

400 g (14 oz) 2 cups dried navy beans, soaked overnight in plenty of water

3 tbsp olive oil

1 red onion, diced

2 garlic cloves, chopped

125 ml (4 fl oz/½ cup) tomato passata

2 tbsp flaxseed meal

1 tsp unrefined salt

SEVEN-SPICE SEASONING

2 tsp smoked paprika

2 tsp ground cumin

1 tsp freshly ground black pepper

1 tsp ground coriander

½ tsp ground cinnamon

½ tsp ground nutmeg

¼ tsp ground cardamom

¼ tsp ground cloves

1 Combine the seven-spice seasoning ingredients in a small bowl then store in an airtight jar for up to 3 months.

2 Drain the beans and place in a large saucepan. Add enough boiling water to cover and bring to the boil. Reduce the heat to low and gently simmer for about 30 minutes or until tender.

3 Meanwhile, heat the oil in a frying pan over medium heat, add the onion and garlic and sauté for 10 minutes, stirring occasionally, until the onion is caramelised.

4 Tip the onion mixture into the pan with the beans and cook slowly for 20 minutes. Stir in the passata, 1 teaspoon of the seven-spice seasoning, flaxseed meal and salt and continue to cook for 15 minutes until all the ingredients are combined and the beans are quite soft.

VEGETABLES

ROAST VEGGIES WITH MAPLE LEMON SAUCE

GF DF VG V SF NF

There's no need to peel veggies if they're organic, as most of the nutrients are in the skin or just under it, but you do need to clean them. If you don't have a veggie scrubber, I recommend you get one. You should be able to find one in your health food or homewares store.

1 parsnip, quartered

1 sweet potato, halved and quartered

2 small corn cobs, halved

4 small potatoes, quartered

2 small fennel bulbs, halved

4 large portobello mushrooms

2 cups 4-cm (1½-in) chunks Japanese pumpkin

2 small red onions, peeled and quartered

1 garlic bulb, cut in half horizontally

125 ml (4 fl oz/½ cup) olive oil

2 tbsp thyme sprigs

2 rosemary sprigs

2 tsp unrefined salt

cracked black pepper

1 handful of flat-leaf parsley leaves, to serve

MAPLE LEMON SAUCE

2 tbsp lemon juice

4 tbsp small capers, chopped

2 tsp pure maple syrup

1 tsp dijon mustard

1 Preheat your oven to 190°C (375°F/Gas 5).

2 Place all the veggies with the garlic, cut side down, on a large baking tray and add the oil, thyme, rosemary and seasoning. Use your hands to rub the seasoning all over the veggies. Transfer to the oven and roast for 20 minutes. Remove the corn, mushrooms and garlic and place on a lovely serving platter.

3 Turn the veggies on the tray and return to the oven for another 15–25 minutes until cooked and golden.

4 For the sauce, whisk all the ingredients together in a small bowl or combine in a small jar and shake. Pour into a jug.

5 Once the veggies are cooked, combine with those on your platter and scatter on the parsley. Serve with the dressing on the side.

VARIATION

✓ For a creamy dressing, whisk 95 g (3¼ oz/⅓ cup) quark or plain yoghurt into the dressing.

BALINESE CABBAGE AND COCONUT SALAD

GF DF VG V SF GrF

This salad is a perfect accompaniment at a barbecue. The divine and fresh Asian flavours lend themselves perfectly to skewers and that smoky barbie flavour.

¼ small cabbage, shredded

1 cup chopped baby spinach leaves or silverbeet

115 g (4 oz/1 cup) bean sprouts

1 tbsp desiccated coconut

2 tbsp roasted peanuts (optional)

1 long red chilli, halved lengthways, deseeded and sliced

DRESSING

4 garlic cloves, crushed

1 long red chilli, thinly sliced

juice of 3 limes

1 lemongrass stem, white part only, thinly sliced

pinch of unrefined salt and cracked black pepper

½ tsp coconut palm sugar

1 tbsp coconut oil

1 Blanch the cabbage in a saucepan of boiling water for 1 minute, then take out and place on a clean tea towel and gently pat dry. Blanch the spinach or silverbeet for 15 seconds and pat dry in a clean tea towel.

2 Wash and drain the bean sprouts.

3 Place the coconut in a frying pan and toast over medium heat until golden and nutty. Remove and set aside.

4 In a bowl, mix together the cabbage, spinach or silverbeet, sprouts, coconut, peanut, if using, and chilli.

5 For the dressing, mix all the ingredients together, then pour over the veggies, toss and serve.

VARIATIONS

✔ Add:

5-cm (2-in) piece of galangal, peeled and grated.

1 tsp coconut vinegar to the dressing.

185 g (6½ oz) 1 cup thinly sliced (use a mandoline) green mango or papaya.

SWEET POTATO FRITTERS

GF V NF

I like to freeze these fritters, then pull them out about an hour before I want them. This sauce, by the way, is something a little bit special, and it's very versatile. Also check out the variations for a bulkier fritter.

1 kg (2 lb 4 oz) sweet potato, cut into chunks

2 tsp tamari

2 tbsp brown rice flour

2 spring onions, thinly sliced

1 tsp sliced red chilli (optional)

1 tbsp rice bran, coconut or olive oil

250 ml (9 fl oz/1 cup) Lemony quark sauce (page 171)

1   Steam your sweet potato until tender, then drain in a colander for at least 5 minutes – an hour is better.

2   In a bowl mash together the sweet potato, tamari, flour, spring onion and chilli, if using, being careful not to overmix. Add more flour if the mixture is too wet – it should be firm and sticky. Shape into 12 fritters about 5 cm (2 in) in diameter and 1 cm (½ in) thick.

3   Heat the oil in a heavy-based frying pan over medium heat. Cook the fritters in batches to prevent them from stewing. You want them nice and crispy. Fry on each side for a few minutes until golden. Serve with the lemony quark sauce.

VARIATIONS

✔ Use coconut, spelt or besan flour instead of the brown rice flour.

✔ Add 1 tsp each ground cumin and turmeric and/or ½ tsp ground coriander to the fritters.

✔ Add 1 cup chopped kale to your sweet potato a few minutes before it's tender.

✔ Add 185 g (6½ oz/1 cup) cooked quinoa to the mixture before shaping into fritters.

SPUDS WITH ZA'ATAR

GF V SF NF GrF

Za'atar, a Middle Eastern spice blend, is made up of sumac, dried oregano and sesame seeds. You can find it in grocery stores, health food stores and Lebanese grocers, or make it yourself. Floury potatoes, like King Edward, Dutch Cream or Sebago are the best varieties for frying and roasting.

4 large potatoes, cut into wedges

3 tbsp olive oil

1 tsp unrefined salt

2 tsp za'atar

2 tbsp roughly chopped mint leaves

plain yoghurt, to serve

grated zest of 1 lemon

1 Preheat your oven to 200°C (400°F/Gas 6).

2 Place the potatoes in a saucepan of cold water and bring to the boil, then reduce the heat to low and simmer for 15 minutes until tender when pierced with a skewer or knife. Drain and pat dry with paper towel.

3 Pour 2 tablespoons of oil into a roasting tin and pop in the oven to get hot for 5 minutes.

4 Toss the spuds in a bowl with the salt, za'atar and the reserved oil. Tip into the hot roasting tin (be careful) and roast, turning once, for 40 minutes or until golden. Serve with the mint sprinkled over the spuds, and the yoghurt and lemon zest mixed together on the side.

VARIATIONS

✔ Instead of the yoghurt try these spuds with Lemony quark sauce (page 171) or Tahini dressing (page 160).

✔ Use sumac instead of za'atar.

JAPANESE FERMENTED VEGGIES

GF DF VG V SF NF GrF R

This is a quick and easy way to prepare the sometimes mysterious fermented vegetable. Discovering the art of fermentation is truly a marvellous thing. Not many other foods (if any) can supply us with vitamin K2, which has been shown to kill cancer cells. Also try other veggies like cucumber or daikon (white radish). Add 1 teaspoon or so to the side of almost any dish. Have them for breakfast with Quinoa breakfast patties (page 10), with your One-egg omelette (page 12), Fried rice (page 62), in your wraps with Tamari tempeh sticks (page 140), or on a cracker with Tahini dressing (page 160).

300 g (10½ oz/4 cups) shaved or shredded cabbage

2 carrots, grated or julienned

1 onion, finely diced

1 tbsp seaweed (such as dulse or nori flakes)

1 tbsp unrefined salt

2 tbsp sake, and extra to store

1 In a large bowl, combine the veggies and seaweed then, using your fingertips, rub in the salt and stir through sake. Cover with a stainless steel or glass lid, or a plate, and place a weight – like a tin of chickpeas – on top. Allow them to pickle overnight at room temperature, or leave for a few days like this, then store in the fridge in a sterilised airtight container for a few months. Make sure the veggies are covered with liquid. Use extra sake if need be.

13.3.14

CARROTS WITH SESAME DRESSING

GF DF VG V NF GrF

Grinding sesame seeds is something that we do far too little. It gives you a texture and nuttiness like nothing else.

1 large carrot

1 tbsp tamari

1 tbsp mirin

2 tbsp white sesame seeds, ground

1   Cut the carrot into matchsticks or half moons and simmer in a saucepan with 4 tablespoons water over medium heat for 2–3 minutes, keeping a crunch in them. Drain (save the water for stock or drink it warm), then return the carrots to the pan.

2   Meanwhile, combine the remaining ingredients in a bowl, pour into the pan and toss to dress the carrots, then serve.

VARIATIONS

✓ Add 1 tsp sake to the dressing.

✓ Use 1½ cups blanched English or Japanese spinach instead of the carrots.

✓ To serve, sprinkle with toasted sesame seeds.

CHINESE MUSHROOMS

GF DF VG V SF NF GrF

Shaoxing rice wine is aged for ten or more years and resembles the taste of dry sherry,
so you can use this as a substitute if you can't find shaoxing.

4 tbsp dried porcini mushrooms

125 ml (4 fl oz/½ cup) boiling water

1 tsp olive oil

2 cups quartered fresh shiitake mushrooms

2 cups button mushrooms, halved

2 cups oyster mushrooms

½ tsp each unrefined salt and cracked black pepper

2 tsp shaoxing rice wine

1   Place the porcini mushrooms in a small bowl, pour over the boiling water and leave to soften, about 5 minutes. Drain, reserve the soaking liquid, and roughly chop.

2   Heat the oil in a large heavy-based frying pan over medium heat. Add all the mushrooms and season, then stir. Cover with a lid, and allow to gently cook for 5–7 minutes. Take the lid off, add the rice wine and the reserved porcini soaking liquid and simmer, uncovered, for 2 minutes, to allow the liquid to reduce a little. Taste and adjust the seasoning to how you like it.

VARIATIONS

✓ Use any mushrooms you like.

✓ Bake in a casserole dish in the oven at 180°C (350°F/Gas 4) for 40 minutes or stir-fry, starting with a little oil, then add 1 tsp each of grated fresh garlic and ginger.

✓ Serve with sliced spring onion and toasted sesame seeds.

ITALIAN MUSHROOMS

GF V SF NF GrF

This dish is, quite frankly, divine, and you don't necessarily need the marjoram and thyme to make it so – but they help.

1 tbsp olive oil

4 large portobello mushrooms

2–3 garlic cloves, crushed

1 tbsp thyme sprigs

2 tbsp marjoram leaves

1 tbsp thinly sliced preserved lemon or grated lemon zest

2 tbsp soft goat's feta

1 tsp truffle oil

1   Heat your oil in a heavy-based frying pan over medium–low heat, add the mushrooms and cook slowly for 5 minutes, turning once. Stir in the garlic and herbs and continue to cook for another minute.

2   Turn off the heat, sprinkle on the lemon and then dollop on the feta. Serve drizzled with the truffle oil.

VARIATIONS

✔ Use buffalo mozzarella, pecorino, taleggio, pecorino or quark instead of the feta.

✔ Any herb, like parsley, basil, chervil, chives or tarragon, will work nicely.

✔ Serve with Creamy corn polenta (page 119).

✔ Use as a topping for Polenta pizza (page 60).

✔ Serve with Tahini dressing (page 160) or Lemony quark sauce (page 171).

✔ Splash in 1 tbsp white wine or verjuice when the mushies are almost cooked, then allow them to simmer for another minute.

✔ Serve on 185 g (6½ oz/1 cup) cooked barley, brown rice or quinoa, or stir it through in the pan.

VIETNAMESE COLESLAW

GF DF VG V SF NF GrF R

A mandoline is a handy gadget in the kitchen, and I'm not a gadget kind of girl. It makes the business of shaving and shredding veggies super-fast, plus it gets them much finer than most of us could manage with a knife. Perfect for coleslaw.

DRESSING

125 ml (4 fl oz/½ cup) water

1 tbsp coconut palm sugar

juice of 2 limes

1 long red chilli, chopped

1 garlic clove, chopped

SALAD

2 tbsp sesame seeds

½ small wombok (Chinese cabbage), shredded

1 carrot, grated

1 red onion, thinly sliced

115 g (4 oz/1 cup) bean sprouts

1 cup shredded or sliced green papaya or mango

10 g (¼ oz/1 cup) Vietnamese mint leaves

1 For the dressing, blitz all the ingredients together in a blender. Set aside.

2 For the salad, combine all the ingredients in a large bowl, then mix in the dressing and toss.

VARIATIONS

✓ Add 1 tbsp fish sauce to the dressing.

✓ Sprinkle with 50 g (1¾ oz/⅓ cup) organic peanuts.

✓ Serve with barbecued kingfish cutlets or chicken thigh fillets. Season your fish or chicken well, then place on a hot, oiled barbie hotplate or in a cast-iron frying pan. Cook the fish for about 2 minutes on each side; the chicken for about 6 minutes on each side. Drain on paper towel.

CREAMY CORN POLENTA

GF V SF NF

Ever thought of making your own polenta? Well, here's how. Serve it whenever you would otherwise have mashed potato, rice or quinoa. It's so very delicious with Italian mushrooms (page 117) and a drizzle of truffle oil.

500 ml (17 fl oz/2 cups) water

6 corn cobs

130 g (4¾ oz/1 cup) crumbled goat's feta

unrefined salt and cracked black pepper

1 Fill a large saucepan with the water, bring to the boil and add the corn cobs. Simmer for only a couple of minutes until the kernels turn a deeper yellow. Remove from the water and, when cool enough to handle, remove the kernels with a sharp knife. Reserve the cooking water.

2 Place the kernels in a blender or food processor and blitz with a little of the reserved cooking water for a minute or two or until you get a smoothish paste, then add more of the liquid to create a wet paste. Return the paste to the pan with the rest of the cooking liquid. Place over low heat and stir with a wooden spoon until warmed through and the consistency of mashed potato. Fold through the feta and season to taste.

VARIATIONS

✔ Leave out the feta and pepper and spread the polenta out on a heatproof dish, then top with the feta and pepper. Place under a hot grill until the feta starts to melt. Top with Italian mushrooms and a few flat-leaf parsley leaves or thyme sprigs.

✔ Serve with Phoenician casserole (page 87).

POACHED VEGGIES

GF DF VG V SF NF GrF

These veggies are gorgeous for a dinner party. A sophisticated dish alone, you may also like to serve this with Tahini dressing (page 160), Aioli (page 165), Tartare sauce (page 165, Variations), Lemony quark sauce (page 171), Almond pesto (page 45) or Broccoli and mint pesto (page 55).

4 baby carrots

2 baby fennel bulbs

½ red onion, quartered

2 celery stalks, cut into batons

1 bunch of asparagus

2 baby zucchini

500 ml (17 fl oz/2 cups) white wine

250 ml (9 fl oz/1 cup) olive oil

juice of ½ lemon

2 bay leaves

1 tbsp peppercorns, any colour

1 tsp unrefined salt

2 tbsp dill tips, to serve

1   Use a veggie scrubber to clean your veg. Trimming only where necessary, cut the veggies into similar-sized pieces.

2   Pour the wine into a deep frying pan over medium heat and simmer for a couple of minutes, then add the oil, lemon juice, bay leaves, peppercorns and salt. Bring back to a simmer, add the carrot and fennel and poach for a couple of minutes, then add the onion and celery and poach for 2 more minutes. Finally, add the asparagus and zucchini and poach for 1 more minute. Be sure you don't overcook them. You want them to keep their colour and still have a little crunch.

3   Using a slotted spoon or tongs, transfer the veggies to a large platter, then spoon some of the poaching liquid over the top. Finish with some dill tips.

4   Keep the liquid in an airtight container in the fridge for up to a week and use for poaching pretty much anything, or freeze for 3 months.

VARIATION

✓ Use the liquid to poach sustainable fish fillets such as wild barramundi, or chicken thigh fillets.

WINTER PUMPHIN

GF DF VG V SF GrF

Why not keep this comforting dish on the baking tray to serve?

2 tbsp olive oil, plus 2 tsp extra for greasing

1 butternut pumpkin

2 tbsp cardamom pods

1 tsp allspice

1–2 tsp unrefined salt

½ small red onion, thinly sliced

45 g (1¾ oz/1 cup) chopped coriander or basil leaves

⅓ cup Cashew cream cheese (page 166)

lime wedges, to serve

1. Preheat the oven to 200°C (400°F/Gas 6). Grease a baking tray with the extra oil.

2. Cut the pumpkin in half lengthways, then slice crossways into 2-cm (¾-in) thick pieces.

3. Bruise the cardamom pods with the side of a knife or smash them open using a mortar and pestle. Discard the pods and grind the seeds to a powder.

4. Mix the ground cardamom with the allspice, oil and salt.

5. Place the pumpkin on the prepared tray, then brush or toss in the oil and spice mixture. Roast for 10–15 minutes until golden and tender. Scatter on the onion and coriander or basil, dollop on blobs of the cashew cream cheese and serve with the lime wedges.

VARIATIONS

✓ Use Tahini dressing (page 160) or Lemony quark sauce (page 171) instead of cashew cream cheese.

✓ Pomegranate seeds make a lovely garnish.

NASU DENGAKU

GF DF VG V NF

Here's the healthy and sustainable version of the yummy baked eggplant with miso sauce you've had at Japanese restaurants and wished you knew how to make at home.

2 large eggplants

4 tbsp olive oil

unrefined salt

2 tbsp black or white sesame seeds

2 spring onions, thinly sliced

MISO SAUCE

2 tbsp shiro miso

1 tbsp rapadura or coconut palm
   sugar

2 tsp sesame oil

1 tbsp mirin

1 tbsp sake

1 Preheat the oven to 200°C (400°F/Gas 6).

2 Cut the eggplants, including the stalks, in half lengthways, then place on a baking tray. Using a small sharp knife, score the cut side of the eggplant in a criss-cross pattern without cutting the skin. Repeat at an angle so you get diamond shapes. Brush with the olive oil until all of it has been absorbed. Sprinkle with some salt and bake for about 40 minutes until golden brown. Remove from the oven and allow to cool slightly.

3 In the meantime, make the sauce by mixing together the miso, sugar, sesame oil, mirin and sake.

4 Brush the sauce generously over the cut side of the eggplant. Pop back in the oven for about 5 minutes until the sauce starts to bubble a little. Serve with the sesame seeds and spring onion scattered on top.

SIDES

TOFU GRILLED IN MISO

GF DF VG V NF GrF

This is a delicious way to prepare tofu. I like to bake it in a shallow dish so the sauce bakes into the tofu, making it nicely golden on top. Place in the oven when you're roasting vegetables or at other times when the oven is already in use. Try using karengo fronds, powdered nori or dulse flakes for the seaweed.

125 ml (4 fl oz/½ cup) white miso

2 tbsp hulled tahini

1½ tbsp mirin

1 × 350 g (12 oz) block firm tofu, cut into 8 pieces

1 tbsp thinly sliced lemon zest

1 tbsp seaweed flakes

1 Preheat your oven to 240°C (475°F/Gas 8).

2 In a small bowl, mix together the miso, tahini and mirin, then pour over the tofu.

3 Place the tofu on a baking tray or in an ovenproof serving dish and bake for 10 minutes or until starting to brown a little around the edges. Finish with the lemon zest and seaweed.

MILLET, CHIA AND FETA FINGERS

GF V SF NF

There are a couple of steps to these incredibly creamy, crunchy, delightful fingers, but I tell you, it's worth it. Prepare the mixture the day before so it is nice and firm for the fingers. These are lovely any time you'd otherwise have baked chips or mash.

210 g (7½ oz/1 cup) millet

2 tbsp chia seeds

1 large potato, peeled and grated or diced

375 ml (13 fl oz/1½ cups) vegetable stock

unrefined salt

65 g (2½ oz/½ cup) crumbled goat's feta

olive oil, for brushing

1   Wash your millet well, then drain. Place in a saucepan and add the chia seeds, potato, stock and salt (or not, depending on how salty your stock is). Half cover the pan with a lid, then bring to the boil. Reduce the heat to medium–low and simmer for 20–25 minutes until the millet is tender. Remove from the heat, secure the lid and allow to rest for a few minutes.

2   Whip the feta into the millet mixture with a wooden spoon, then taste for seasoning. Pour onto a greased or lined 30-cm × 40-cm (12-in × 16-in) baking tray and flatten out with wet hands or a spatula. Allow to cool a little, then cover and place in the fridge to set for a couple of hours or overnight.

3   Preheat the oven to 180°C (350°F/Gas 4). When the millet mixture is firm, cut into rectangles about 3 cm × 10 cm (1¼-in × 4 in), then brush with the olive oil. Bake, flipping once, until both sides are golden, about 20 minutes. Alternatively, shallow- or deep-fry in coconut oil.

VARIATIONS

✓ Brush the fingers with olive oil, then grill instead of baking.

✓ Serve as a mash (pictured) after whipping in the feta. Use this any time you would serve mash. Try it with fresh salads or sautéed Asian greens.

FLATBREAD

V SF NF

Many of us are avoiding bread, as we're finding it just too difficult to digest. More and more of us are avoiding it due to an allergy to gluten. If you can eat a little gluten then this bread (pictured on page 16) is for you. It's thin and made with the easier to digest spelt flour. Have it with breakfast, dips, soups or Chopped salad with black beans and pomegranate molasses (page 30). Using a rolling pin, roll out your dough so that it's nice and thin.

75 g (2½ oz/½ cup) wholemeal spelt flour

130 g (4¾ oz/½ cup) Greek yoghurt

25 g (1 oz/½ cup) finely chopped coriander leaves

1½ tsp baking powder

½ tsp unrefined salt

1 tbsp olive oil

1 In a bowl, combine the flour, yoghurt, coriander, baking powder and salt and, using your hands, mix to form a dry dough. Add more flour if needed. Knead for 1–2 minutes until smooth.

2 Wrap the dough in a tea towel or place in a container and seal, then chill in the fridge for 30 minutes.

3 Divide the mixture into 6 portions, roll each portion into a ball, then flatten and roll out to form a thin disc about 2 mm (1/16 in) thick.

4 Brush the oil over a heavy-based frying pan or griddle over medium heat. Depending on the size, add your flatbread 1 or 3 at a time, then fry for 2 minutes on each side until golden.

VARIATIONS

✔ Sprinkle ½ tsp cumin seeds or poppy seeds onto the flattened dough before cooking.

✔ Use any other herbs like dill, mint, basil, parsley or chives instead of the coriander.

✔ Cook the flatbread on the barbie, on a hotplate or in a chargrill pan.

YUBA SPRING ROLLS

GF DF VG V NF GrF

Bean curd skins, 'yuba' in Japanese, are made from the dried skin that forms as soy milk is boiled. If the skins are stiff and tend to crack easily, moisten them slightly with a damp tea towel before using them as wrappers. You can also use spring roll wrappers but they contain white flour.

1 tbsp coconut or olive oil

2 garlic cloves, crushed

1 tsp grated fresh ginger

1 small potato, diced

1 small carrot, diced

1 tbsp water

95 g (3¼ oz/½ cup) diced firm tofu

2 tsp Thai curry paste

1 × 50 g (1¾ oz) bundle of rice vermicelli, soaked in hot water for 2 minutes

1 tbsp tamari

1 tsp sesame oil

2 spring onions, finely chopped

15 g (½ oz/½ cup) coriander leaves, plus extra to serve

1 × 200 g (7 oz) packet 20-cm (8-in) square bean curd skins

FLOUR PASTE

1 tbsp gluten-free flour mixed with 1 tbsp water

DIPPING SAUCE

2 tbsp tamari

few drops of sesame oil

4 tbsp coconut or macadamia oil for shallow-frying or 1 cup to deep-fry

- ✓ Instead of using a ready-made curry paste, use 1 crushed garlic clove, 1 tsp each of grated fresh ginger and turmeric and 1 tsp five-spice.

- ✓ Add 3 fresh shiitake mushies or 3 rehydrated dried ones, stems removed and caps sliced.

- ✓ Add 1 tsp rice vinegar.

- ✓ Add 4 peeled and finely chopped green prawns, 50 g (1¾ oz) shredded cooked chicken or the same amount of crabmeat.

- ✓ Add 1 tbsp arame, powdered nori or dulse flakes when sautéing your veggies.

- ✓ You can use other veggies like corn, sliced beans or peas.

- ✓ Add 1 tsp grated ginger to the dipping sauce.

- ✓ The spring rolls can also be steamed in a bamboo steamer, or brushed with a little macadamia or coconut oil and baked at 180°C (350°F/Gas 4) for 10–15 minutes.

1 Heat the oil in a heavy-based frying pan over medium heat, add your garlic, ginger and veggies and sauté, stirring occasionally, for 2 minutes or until starting to soften. Add the water and cook for another minute. Now add the tofu and curry paste, stir well to coat, and cook until the curry paste starts to stick to the bottom of the pan. Add a splash more water.

2 Drain and roughly chop your noodles, then add to the pan along with the tamari, sesame oil, spring onion and coriander. Stir well and taste for seasoning.

3 Preheat the oven to 100°C (200°F/Gas ½).

4 To make the spring rolls, place a bean curd skin on a work surface, spoon a tablespoonful of the veggie mixture in a line near the edge closest to you. Brush the top and edges of the bean curd skin with the flour paste, then roll up, tucking in the edges as you go. Repeat with the remaining skins and filling.

5 Place a wok or heavy-based frying pan over high heat and pour in oil to a depth of 3 cm (1¼ in). Don't let the oil get so hot that it 'smokes'. Carefully add the bean curd rolls, being careful not to overcrowd the pan. Put less rather than more in. Cook for 2 minutes on each side until golden brown. Drain on paper towel.

6 Transfer the spring rolls to a heatproof dish and keep warm in the oven while cooking the remaining rolls.

7 For the dipping sauce, combine the tamari and sesame oil in a small serving bowl and mix well.

8 Place the spring rolls on a platter, sprinkle on the extra coriander leaves and serve with the dipping sauce.

YELLOW COCONUT RICE

GF DF VG V SF NF

Organic or pesticide-free brown rice is just sooo much nicer than conventionally farmed rice. It's soft, fluffy and doesn't taste and feel like birdseed. No wonder so many say they don't like brown rice – it's probably because they haven't tasted the fresh, young and clean stuff. Serve this Asian-inspired salad with the Balinese cabbage and coconut salad (page 109) and Indonesian salad (page 21).

2 tbsp coconut or sesame oil

3 French shallots, diced or sliced

2 garlic cloves, chopped

400 g (14 oz/2 cups) long-grain brown rice, rinsed

625 ml (21½ fl oz/2½ cups) or 1 × 400 ml (14 fl oz) BPA-free tin coconut milk

500 ml (17 fl oz/2 cups) vegetable stock or water

1 tbsp grated fresh turmeric or 2 tsp ground turmeric

2 kaffir lime or curry leaves

2 long red chillies, halved lengthways, deseeded and sliced, to serve

1 Heat the oil in a heavy-based saucepan over medium heat, add the shallot and garlic and cook until just starting to change colour. Add the rice and stir to coat in the oil. Stir in the coconut milk, stock or water, turmeric and lime or curry leaves. Bring to the boil, reduce the heat to low, cover with the lid and cook for 15–20 minutes until the liquid has been absorbed. Turn off the heat, keep covered and leave the rice to steam for another 15 or so minutes.

2 Fluff up the rice with a fork and serve with the chilli scattered on top.

VARIATIONS

✓ Add 1 tsp unrefined salt if using water instead of stock.

✓ Stir in 1 tbsp grated fresh ginger with the shallot and garlic.

BLACK BEAN TOFU

GF DF VG V NF GrF

I wrote this recipe while on a seven-day fast in Bali, and remember thinking how fantastic it sounded, but wondered if that was only because I was starving. No, is the answer. This is amazing.

1 × 300 g (10½ oz) block firm tofu, cut into 3-cm (1¼-in) cubes

60 g (2¼ oz/½ cup) gluten-free cornflour or coconut flour

125 ml (4 fl oz/½ cup) macadamia or coconut oil

4 spring onions, thinly sliced

BLACK BEAN SAUCE

4 tbsp macadamia or coconut oil

6 French shallots, thinly sliced

4 long red chillies, thinly sliced

6 garlic cloves, crushed

1 tbsp grated fresh ginger

1 × 400 g (14 oz) BPA-free tin black beans, drained and rinsed

4 tbsp tamari

1 tbsp rice syrup or pure maple syrup

2 tbsp black peppercorns, crushed

1   Pat the tofu dry with paper towel, then coat in the flour, shaking off any excess.

2   Heat a wok or heavy-based frying pan with deep sides over medium–high heat and pour in the oil to a depth of 3 cm (1¼ in). Carefully add the tofu, being sure not to overcrowd the pan, and fry, turning it over so it becomes golden on all sides. This will take around 5 minutes. Remove from the pan and drain on paper towel.

3   Discard the oil in the pan and wipe clean with paper towel.

4   For the black bean sauce, heat the same pan over medium heat and pour in the oil. Add the shallot, chilli, garlic and ginger and sauté, stirring occasionally, for about 5 minutes until soft. Add the black beans, tamari and syrup and stir again. Add the crushed peppercorns and stir again with a fork, gently crushing some of the beans. You may want to add a little water if the sauce is too thick.

5   Return the tofu to the pan and spoon over the sauce. Finish with the spring onion.

VARIATIONS

✓ Try using silken instead of firm tofu. Be very gentle with it as it breaks easily.

✓ Use raw honey instead of rice or maple syrup for a sweeter finish.

SNACKS

TAMARI TEMPEH STICKS

GF DF VG V NF GrF

Tempeh is a fermented soy product so it is easier to digest than tofu. It's also a good source of vitamin B12 and protein. I'm partial to the organic chickpea flavour that Byron Bay Tempeh do so well, but if you can't find that one, try any organic brand. Cut it into fingers or small wedges and deep- or shallow-fry, bake or grill, ready for tossing in stir-fries, wraps, curries or salads or putting straight into the lunchbox for a snack.

1 × 300 g (10½ oz) block tempeh

coconut oil

2 tsp tamari

1   Slice the tempeh into 1-cm (½-in) thick pieces. Heat your oil (up to you how much you use) in a heavy-based frying pan and add the tempeh. Cook on both sides for about 2 minutes until golden brown all over.

2   Drain on paper towel then transfer to a serving plate and drizzle with a little tamari. Set aside to marinate for a minute or two then tuck in.

VARIATIONS

✓ Grill or bake the tempeh instead.

✓ Cut the tempeh into any size or shape you like, then add more oil to the pan and deep-fry. Drain on paper towel.

✓ Press the tempeh into blitzed cornflakes (from a health food store) or breadcrumbs made by processing leftover bread, and cook in coconut or macadamia oil.

✓ Serve with Aioli (page 165), Cocktail sauce (page 165, Variations) or Tartare sauce (page 165, Variations).

SWEET CHOCOLATE ALMONDS

GF DF VG V SF GrF

Cacao butter is obtained from whole cacao beans that have been fermented, roasted and separated from their hulls, which are used to make cacao powder. Available from health food stores and delis, it's worth spending the extra money to buy organic cacao butter, otherwise you may be using a product that's been deodorised to neutralise its strong taste and smell.

160 g (5¾ oz/1 cup) whole almonds

1 tbsp coconut flour

40 g (1½ oz/⅓ cup) raw cacao powder

1 tbsp granule sweetener

2 tbsp cacao butter, softened

1 Preheat your oven to 180°C (350°F/Gas 4).

2 Mix all the ingredients together in a bowl. Adjust sweetness to your liking, then spread on a baking tray. Bake for 10–15 minutes until golden brown, stirring or shaking once. Store in an airtight container for about 2 weeks. Keep them in the fridge in the warmer months.

VARIATIONS

✔ Use 2 tbsp coconut or macadamia oil instead of the cacao butter.

✔ Try any nut.

✔ Toss in 4 tbsp shredded coconut.

BLISS BALLS

GF DF VG V SF

Perhaps the first recipe I ever wrote, many years ago now, this is definitely one of my most loved and used. I've updated it and added ingredients that weren't as readily available back then. These little balls of goodness are now a whole lot better.

30 g (1 oz/1 cup) puffed millet, amaranth, quinoa or brown rice

50 g (1¾ oz/⅓ cup) sesame seeds

55 g (2 oz/⅓ cup) sunflower seeds

1 cup toasted unsalted chopped nuts (such as almonds, cashews, Brazil nuts, hazelnuts or macadamias)

150 g (5½ oz/1 cup) mixed seeds (such as hemp, chia, sesame, sunflower, pepitas or flaxseed meal)

1 cup flaked, shredded or desiccated coconut

1 cup chopped dried fruit (such as apricots, apples, peaches, pears, raisins, dates or goji berries)

205–270 g (7¼–9½ oz/¾–1 cup) hulled tahini

260–350 g (9¼–12 oz/¾–1 cup) rice syrup

½ cup sesame seeds, hemp seeds, raw cacao powder and/or shredded or desiccated coconut, for rolling

1   Place all the dry ingredients in a food processor and blitz until still a bit chunky. Transfer to a large bowl.

2   Add the dried fruit to the food processor and blitz, keeping the texture a bit chunky. Add to the dry ingredients in the bowl, then mix together. Return this mixture to the food processor (you may have to do this in batches) and, while the motor is running, gradually pour in the tahini and rice syrup and process until a shiny ball forms. Taste the mixture and adjust the sweetness and the amount of tahini to your liking.

3   Using wet hands and working with 1 tablespoon of mixture at a time, roll into balls, then coat in either the sesame and/or hemp seeds, cacao powder and/or coconut.

4   Store the balls in an airtight container. They will last for months in the fridge, which keeps them fresher, but they're just as happy in the pantry.

VARIATIONS

✓ Add:

40 g (1½ oz/⅓ cup) raw cacao powder or cacao nibs to the dry ingredients.

2 tbsp coconut, hemp, chia or flaxseed oil with the tahini.

camu camu powder, gubinge powder or other micro greens like spirulina, wheatgrass or barley grass.

✓ Use raw honey or coconut nectar instead of the rice syrup.

ALL SEED CRACKERS

GF DF VG V SF NF GrF

This is one of my favourite and most-made recipes of late. Most crackers are made with grains and sometimes I don't feel like or want grains, so these are perfect. The chia and the flaxseed meal hold them together beautifully. If you use a dehydrator, they'll remain raw, or keep the oven temperature below 50°C (120°F) and cook for three hours. If they're not crunchy enough, flip them over then put them back in for another hour.

50 g (2 oz/⅓ cup) mixed chia and flaxseed meal

⅔ cup mixed hemp, sesame, sunflower, pepitas, nigella and poppy seeds

250 ml (9 fl oz/1 cup) water

1 tsp unrefined salt

1 Preheat the oven to 150°C (300°F/Gas 2). Line a 30-cm × 40-cm (12-in × 16-in) baking tray with baking paper.

2 Place everything in a bowl, then mix well to form a wet dough. Let the dough sit for about 15 minutes to allow the chia to swell up and go gooey.

3 Using wet hands or a spatula, spread the dough out until about 5 mm (¼ in) thick on the prepared tray, then score into sixteen rectangles with a sharp knife. Bake for 1 hour, turn off the oven and leave to dry out in the oven for a further hour. If using a dehydrator, press the dough onto 3 or 4 Teflex sheets, score, then put on 175°C (345°F/Gas 4) for 12 hours. Remove the crackers from the Teflex sheet and cut all the way through to create individual crackers, then place upside down on the sheet and return to the dehydrator for 3 hours.

4 Allow the crackers to cool slightly before storing in an airtight container for up to 1 week. They'll stay fresher for longer in the fridge.

VARIATIONS

✓ Omit the salt and add 2 tsp ground cinnamon or freshly grated nutmeg and 60 g (2¼ oz/½ cup) roughly ground pecans.

✓ For sweet crackers, add 4 tbsp pure maple syrup, 4 tbsp cacao nibs and 1 tsp ground cinnamon.

✓ In a bowl over simmering water melt 55 g (2 oz/½ cup) raw cacao powder together with 125 g (4½ oz/½ cup) cacao butter then leave it to cool. Spread over the top of your crackers and allow to cool. Store in the fridge for a week to 10 days.

COCONUT YOGHURT

GF DF VG V SF NF GrF

This is a lovely dairy-free alternative to yoghurt. I love making this and experimenting with different flavours. You will find both kefir granules and probiotic granules in health food stores.

2 young coconuts

1 tsp lemon juice

½ tsp natural vanilla extract or seeds from 1 vanilla bean, split lengthways

1 sachet of kefir granules or 2 probiotic capsules

1   Open your coconuts by using a large mallet or knife, then drain the liquid out. Reserve the liquid. Scoop out the flesh, pop it into your blender and pour in enough of the coconut liquid to process to a purée. Start with a little while the motor is running, then add a little more at a time. Add the lemon juice, vanilla and kefir and blend again. Taste. Adjust the lemon or vanilla, if you like.

2   Pour the yoghurt into a bowl and cover firmly with a tea towel. Leave in a warm, dry place overnight or for at least 12 hours. It'll keep in the fridge for about 2 weeks.

VARIATIONS

✔ Purée ½ cup mango, berries, papaya, banana or passionfruit pulp and pour into the bowl before pouring the yoghurt on top to set.

✔ To make it sweet, add 1 tbsp maple, rice or coconut syrup or raw honey.

✔ Add 30 g (1 oz/¼ cup) hemp seeds for a little crunch.

✔ Use the grated zest of the lemon as well as the juice.

HERBED SWEET POTATO CHIPS

GF DF VG V SF NF GrF

Just wait until you try these, pictured on page 66. You'll be amazed at how good they are, so make lots! They're also great on the barbie. Sweet potatoes are a valuable source of vitamin A so they're wonderful for your skin and for boosting immunity. They're also packed with antioxidants.

1 small sweet potato

½ tsp curry powder

1 tsp dried thyme

1 tbsp olive or coconut oil

½ tsp unrefined salt

1   Preheat the oven to 190°C (375°F/Gas 5).

2   Use a vegetable peeler to peel the sweet potato into long strips, then cut in half to make smaller pieces. Put them in a bowl and add all the other ingredients. Toss well with your hands or tongs.

3   Place the sweet potato on a baking tray in the oven and cook, turning once, for 15–20 minutes until golden.

4   These chips will keep in an airtight container for a week or so. Just make sure they're completely cool before storing them, otherwise you'll have soggy chips.

SUPER NATURAL FOOD BARS

GF DF VG V SF GrF R

You don't have to use this exact recipe; it's more of a guide. Never again do you need to buy a muesli bar, not once you know how to make these little bars of goodness. Plus there's the added benefit of no packaging. Soaking the nuts and seeds softens them and removes some of the hard-to-digest enzyme inhibitors, making them softer than your usual bars. This is a good way to include spirulina in your diet, other than in your green smoothies.

1 cup pitted dates or dried figs

160 g (5¾ oz/1 cup) whole almonds

75 g (2¾ oz/½ cup) pepitas

30 g (1 oz/¼ cup) hemp seeds

¼ cup spirulina or Lifestream Essential Greens (available from health food stores and pharmacies)

40 g (1½ oz/¼ cup) sunflower seeds

4 tbsp cacao nibs

35 g (1¼ oz/½ cup) shredded coconut

2 tbsp maca powder

3 tbsp coconut oil, plus 3 tbsp extra

1 tsp ground cardamom

1 tsp ground cinnamon

¼ tsp natural vanilla extract

1 Cover the dried fruit, nuts and seeds with water and soak for at least 8 hours. (I soak them in the morning and then make the bars later in the day, or soak overnight and make the bars the next morning.) After soaking, rinse well and drain.

2 Place the soaked dried fruit, nuts and seeds in your food processor and whiz for a minute to make a chunky paste. Then add the remaining ingredients and blitz, scraping down the side once or twice, to form a thick paste that looks like granola. You may need to add a little water. If it's still too dry, add the extra coconut oil and process again. The processing will heat the coconut oil enough to help it blend everything together.

3 Scoop the mixture into a 30-cm × 30-cm (12-in × 12-in) tray and press down firmly and evenly with a spatula or wet hands. Freeze for 30 minutes or refrigerate for 1 hour until firm. Cut into bars while still in the tray and wrap individually in baking paper. These will keep in an airtight container for up to 1 week in the fridge and for up to 1 month in the freezer.

VARIATIONS

✔ Add chia seeds and flaxseed meal or goji berries.

✔ You could also roll the mixture into bite-sized balls.

COCONUT AND CACAO COOKIES

DF VG V SF NF

This is my take on Anzac biscuits. If you aren't a coconut lover then use macadamia oil and leave out the shredded coconut. It's a nice way to use up coconut or almond pulp left over after making milk.

100 g (3½ oz/1 cup) oats

65 g (2½ oz/1 cup) shredded coconut

1 cup cacao nibs

1 tbsp hot water

75 g (2½ oz/⅓ cup) granule sweetener

1 tsp bicarbonate of soda

250 ml (9 fl oz/1 cup) coconut oil

1 Preheat your oven to 190°C (375°F/Gas 5). Grease a baking tray.

2 In a bowl, mix together the oats, coconut and cacao nibs.

3 In a separate bowl, stir together the rest of the ingredients. Pour into the dry ingredients and mix well. Taste, and adjust the flavours to how you like. Drop dessertspoonfuls of the mixture onto the prepared tray and press down slightly with a fork. Bake for 15 minutes or until golden. Cool on a wire rack.

4 These cookies will keep for about a week stored in an airtight container.

VARIATIONS

✔ Add 145 g (5½ oz/1 cup) dried cranberries and halve the amount of granule sweetener.

✔ Use quinoa flakes instead of oats for a gluten-free alternative.

RAW BROWNIES

GF DF VG V SF NF GrF R

I like putting as many superfoods as I can in one dish. This has five! Add some powdered super greens like spirulina or wheatgrass powder for more. Maca is a root veggie from Peru that is used to treat hormonal imbalance and increase energy. It's also loaded with nutrients. It's available in powdered form, and has a malty taste.

8 pitted dates or dried figs

30 g (1 oz/¼ cup) hemp seeds

20 g (¾ oz/¼ cup) chia seeds

¼ cup maca powder

½ tsp ground star anise (optional)

35 g (1¼ oz/½ cup) shredded coconut

1 tsp ground cinnamon

30 g (1 oz/¼ cup) raw cacao powder

grated zest and juice of 1 lemon

1 Cover the dried fruit with water and set aside to soak for about 1 hour. Drain well and place in a food processor with the hemp and chia seeds, maca powder, star anise, if using, coconut, cinnamon and cacao powder. Pulse for 15–20 seconds until a thick dough forms.

2 Transfer to a 24-cm (9½-in) square cake tin and, with wet hands or a spatula, press the mixture down evenly, making sure you get it right to the edges. Squeeze on the lemon juice, sprinkle over the zest and smooth the top.

3 Place the dish in the fridge for an hour, or overnight, to set. Cut into whatever shapes and sizes you want.

VARIATION

✔ Sprinkle on shredded or flaked coconut before the brownie goes in the fridge.

DRESSINGS & SAUCES

TAHINI DRESSING AND HUMMUS

GF DF VG V SF NF GrF

Perhaps I should dedicate an entire book to my love of these two condiments. I get so excited experimenting with new combinations of flavours and, seriously, it never ends. Hummus is simply tahini dressing with chickpeas, and both are something you absolutely must know how to make, and make you will – all the time. Here's my basic recipe followed by some of my favourite variations (page 162). I usually use my Vitamix which gives both tahini dressing and hummus an incredibly smooth and light texture, unless I'm only making a small amount, in which case I do it by hand. Of course use dried chickpeas, soak overnight and then boil until soft if you prefer that to using tins. You'll find the method for doing so on page 100.

4 tbsp hulled tahini

juice of 1 lemon

1 garlic clove

½ tsp unrefined salt

2 tbsp water

1 × 400g (14 oz) BPA-free tin chickpeas, drained (for hummus only)

1 Put all the ingredients in your food processor or blender and blitz until smooth. Taste and adjust the flavours the way you like them. Use as much or as little lemon juice as you need to achieve the consistency you like.

HUMMUS

✔ As on page 160 but add 1 tsp ground cumin.

✔ Using unhulled tahini will keep the recipe raw and make the taste deeper/stronger.

✔ Add:

1 tsp apple cider vinegar, ½ tsp unrefined salt, 1 tsp dulse flakes, water to thin.

2 tbsp hemp seeds and ½ bunch of basil leaves.

2 boiled, peeled and chopped beetroot, ½ cup dill leaves and 1 tsp ground cumin.

1 cup steamed chopped pumpkin and 1 tsp ground cumin.

1 bunch of chopped coriander and 1 tbsp lime juice.

1 chopped kale leaf and 2 tsp grated fresh ginger.

2 tsp each ground fennel and cumin and 130 g (4¾ oz/½ cup) plain yoghurt.

1 tsp smoked paprika and ½ cup roasted capsicum.

1 tbsp harissa paste.

1 tbsp za'atar, ½ cup roasted capsicum and 2 tsp preserved lemon.

1 tbsp grated fresh turmeric.

1 tbsp miso paste.

1 tsp tamari, 2 tsp syrup sweetener, 1 tbsp apple cider vinegar and 1½ tbsp mirin.

1 tbsp shiro miso paste, 1 tsp grated fresh ginger and ½ tsp tamari instead of the salt.

CREAMY WALNUT AND AVOCADO SAUCE

GF DF VG V SF

With a good hit of omega oils in the walnuts and avocado, iron and antioxidants in the greens, and essential fatty acids and calcium in the tahini, this is an easy and awfully yummy way to include superfoods in your diet. Try it mixed through pasta, on toast or drizzled over steamed veggies. It's also pretty special wrapped inside a crepe.

2 cups chopped silverbeet or baby
    spinach leaves

115 g (4 oz/⅓ cup) unsalted walnuts

90 g (3¼ oz/⅓ cup) hulled tahini

½ avocado

½ tsp ground cumin

juice of 1 lemon

6 mint leaves

1 tsp unrefined salt, or to taste

1 Place all the ingredients in a blender or food processor and blitz until combined. I like it so it still has a bit of texture to it, but it's up to you how smooth you make it.

VARIATIONS

✔ Use raw or toasted nuts, but make sure they're unsalted.

✔ Try adding other herbs like basil, flat-leaf parsley or coriander.

✔ Unhulled tahini will make the recipe raw.

FLAVOURED SALT

GF DF VG V SF GrF

As a general rule, use three times the amount of unrefined or Himalayan salt to flavourings. For a longer shelf life, use dried flavourings like herbs, spices and teas. If you want to use fresh ingredients, such as chilli, lemongrass, ginger or herbs, then you'll need to dry them before adding them to the salt, otherwise make only what you need as they won't keep for longer than a few days. To dry them, pound your ingredients together to make a paste, spread out on a baking tray and put in a 110°C (225°F/Gas ¼) oven for around an hour to get rid of all the moisture. (Alternatively, use a dehydrator.) Once they're completely dry, whiz in your food processor, or use a mortar and pestle and store in an airtight container for up to three months. After that the flavours will start to diminish.

160 g (5½ oz/½ cup) unrefined or Himalayan salt

2 tbsp flavourings – select from these ideas:

dried chilli, lemongrass and grated lime zest

fresh rosemary and garlic

jasmine tea leaves

grated lemon zest and vanilla seeds (from a vanilla bean)

fennel seeds and grated lime zest

fresh ginger and fresh chilli, seeds removed

sichuan peppercorns, dried chilli and ginger

fresh rosemary and grated orange zest

sichuan peppercorns and grated lime or mandarin zest

toasted sesame seeds

pistachio nuts and cumin seeds

1 Place the salt in a mortar. Add your flavouring of choice and pound with a pestle until well combined. Store in an airtight container for up to 3 months.

AIOLI

GF DF V SF NF R

This garlic mayonnaise, which is repeatedly requested whenever I have guests, is great with seafood, chicken, lamb or scraped on a wrap before stuffing with roast veggies and greens. To save time, you can buy a whole-egg or organic soy mayo.

MAYONNAISE

2 egg yolks, at room temperature

½ tsp unrefined salt

pinch of cracked white pepper

1 tsp dijon mustard

2 tsp white wine or apple cider vinegar or lemon juice

185 ml (6 fl oz/¾ cup) rice bran, macadamia or unrefined safflower oil

3 tbsp extra virgin olive oil

AIOLI

1 tbsp lemon or lime juice

grated zest of 1 lemon or lime

2 spring onions, finely diced

1–2 garlic cloves, crushed

1 tbsp baby capers

2 tbsp chopped coriander stems and leaves

1   First, make your mayo. In a bowl (or you can do this in a food processor), combine the egg yolks, salt, pepper, mustard and 1 teaspoon of the vinegar or lemon juice and whisk well.

2   Gradually add the oil, drop by drop, whisking constantly and making sure each addition is thoroughly incorporated before adding the next. As the mixture thickens, the oil flow can be increased to a steady thin stream, but keep whisking until emulsified. When all the oil has been added, whisk in the remaining vinegar or lemon juice. Store in the fridge in a covered jar for up to a week.

3   To make the aioli, spoon about 1 cup of your mayo into a bowl and add the lemon or lime juice and zest.

4   On a chopping board or using a mortar and pestle, make a paste out of the spring onion, garlic, capers and coriander stems and leaves, and add this to the mayo. Stir well. Taste, and adjust the seasoning to how you like it.

VARIATIONS

✓ For **Tartare sauce**, add 1 tbsp diced dill pickles and 1 tbsp dill to ½ cup aioli.

✓ For **Cocktail sauce**, add 1 tsp tomato paste or 1 tbsp tomato passata and juice from a lime to ½ cup mayonnaise.

✓ For **Lime mayonnaise**, use the juice and grated zest of a lime in the mayo in place of the vinegar or lemon juice. Nice also with 1 tbsp chopped coriander leaves.

✓ For **Sesame mayonnaise**, add a few drops of sesame oil and 1 tbsp lightly ground toasted sesame seeds to the mayo.

CASHEW CREAM CHEESE

GF DF VG V SF GrF R

Some people use nutritional yeast to make this 'cheese', but I'm not a fan, plus you get plenty of flavour by using the vinegar and mustard. The first time I made this I was surprised at just how delicious it was – and I still am each time I make it. Cashews are such a great source of niacin, which helps to treat anxiety and depression, and eating this sauce, well, it just makes you happy.

155 g (5½ oz/1 cup) raw cashews, soaked in 375 ml (13 fl oz/1½ cups) water for an hour

1 tsp grated lemon zest

1 tbsp lemon juice

2 tsp apple cider vinegar

1 garlic clove (optional)

1 tbsp dijon mustard

1 tsp each unrefined salt and cracked white pepper

1   Drain your cashews, then place in a blender with the other ingredients and blitz until thick and luscious. You may want to adjust the flavours to your liking. It will firm up when chilled for a couple of hours, making it easier to spread. Leave out of the fridge until it softens a little if you want to use it on pasta or as a sauce. It will last for about 1 week, stored in an airtight container in the fridge.

VARIATION

✓   Use 1 tbsp shiro miso instead of the mustard and salt and pepper.

CHOCOLATE COCONUT SPREAD

GF DF VG V SF NF GrF R

Nutella is Australia's number one-selling spread, but it is loaded with sugar and other scary things. It'll take you only a couple of minutes to whiz up this gorgeous spread and you'll be so very glad you did. Mix a teaspoon with hot almond milk for a wintry nightcap, spread it on chunky bread with macadamia butter, thin it out with a little liqueur and have it in a crepe, use as icing on cupcakes, or melt it and pour over fruit. Or there's always the option of a spoon in a jar in the pantry.

125 g (4½ oz/½ cup) coconut butter
125 ml (4 fl oz/½ cup) coconut oil
55 g (2 oz/½ cup) raw cacao powder
90 g (3¼ oz/¼ cup) syrup sweetener
¼ tsp unrefined salt

1   Gently melt the coconut butter and oil in a small saucepan over low heat. Allow to cool a little, then transfer to a bowl and mix in the rest of the ingredients. Store in an airtight jar for up to 6 months. In the warmer months it'll melt in the pantry, so better to keep it in the fridge then.

VARIATION

✔ Add 2 tsp natural vanilla extract and 185 ml (6 fl oz/¾ cup) coconut cream. In this case it will last about a week in the fridge.

LEMONGRASS DRESSING

GF DF VG V SF NF GrF R

Pour this dressing over steamed veggies, use as a marinade, or as a base for your stir-fries or curries, or serve as a condiment with brown rice and baked veggies.

4 lemongrass stems, white part only, bruised and thinly sliced
4 red Asian shallots, finely chopped
2 garlic cloves, finely chopped
1 bird's eye chilli, thinly sliced
2 kaffir lime leaves, thinly sliced
2 tbsp lime juice
4 tbsp coconut oil
pinch of unrefined salt and cracked black pepper

1   Combine all the ingredients in a bowl and whisk for 5 minutes, or blitz in a food processor or blender until emulsified. It'll keep in the fridge in an airtight container for a week.

VARIATION
✓ Add 3 chopped anchovy fillets.

MISO DIPPING SAUCE

GF DF VG V NF GrF

Make lots of this sauce as you'll find more and more ways to use it. Look for organic miso, which won't be made from GMO soy beans, and one that's preferably Australian, as the effects of the radioactive fallout from the Fukushima disaster are constantly being discovered far and wide. Miso is a wonderful food, loaded with protein and cancer-fighting properties, which helps to balance your gut flora and keep your blood sugar stable.

125 ml (4 fl oz/½ cup) miso
1 tbsp mirin
1 tsp grated fresh ginger
2 tbsp vegetable stock
2 tbsp sesame seeds

1   In a small saucepan over low–medium heat, combine all the ingredients and simmer for 5 minutes, stirring frequently. Cool and store in an airtight container for up to a week in the fridge.

GREEN SAUCE

GF DF VG V SF NF GrF R

Open my fridge and chances are you'll see a large jar of this sauce inside. I go out to the garden, bring back huge amounts of herbs – every kind – and wash them, then into the blender they go, along with the other ingredients. Out comes a bright green heavenly sauce that gets slathered on crackers or wraps. It's also lovely as an accompaniment to veggies, tofu, tempeh or seafood.

1 cup each flat-leaf parsley, coriander and basil leaves

½ cup each tarragon, dill, mint and fennel tips

2 spring onions or French shallots, chopped

1 tbsp dijon mustard

1 tbsp baby capers

2 dill pickles, roughly chopped

1–2 garlic cloves, peeled

1 tbsp apple cider vinegar

125 ml (4 fl oz/½ cup) olive oil

1 tsp unrefined salt, or to taste

1   Blitz everything together in a blender or food processor, scraping down the side, until smooth. Season as you like then store in the fridge in a sterilised airtight jar for a week.

VARIATIONS

✓ Add 2–4 anchovy fillets.

✓ Any vinegar will work.

✓ Also good served with fish or poultry or dolloped on soup.

✓ Leave out the olive oil.

✓ Stir 1 tbsp through curry when you add your stock or water.

✓ Dollop a big spoonful onto cooked quinoa or barley with toasted nuts, a legume and leafy greens.

GREMOLATA

GF DF VG V SF NF GrF R

This is an Italian specialty used to lift a heavy stew. It's so versatile and puts to good use some of my favourite and always-on-hand ingredients – garlic, parsley and lemons. Always use fresh garlic. And when new season garlic is available, grab it. It's at its best around September/October in Australia. I plant a lot, usually at Easter, so I have enough to last all year. The stuff in the supermarket has been dried and bleached and usually requires a long plane trip to get here.

Crushing garlic makes it sweeter and helps to release its healing properties more than chopping will.

Adjust the measurements below to your liking, and if you'd like to make extra and have it on hand at all times, just add enough extra virgin olive oil to cover the top.

15 g (½ oz/½ cup) finely chopped
    flat-leaf parsley

1 tsp grated lemon zest

1 garlic clove, crushed

unrefined salt

1   In a small bowl, mix all the ingredients together, or you can pound using a mortar and pestle or blitz in a food processor or blender. Store in the fridge in an airtight jar for a week.

VARIATIONS

- ✓ Add dried chilli flakes and olive oil and toss through pasta.
- ✓ Roast a whole bulb of garlic, then mix the softened cloves with the other ingredients for a divine sauce.

FLORAL DRESSING

GF DF VG V SF NF GrF R

Pour this over mixed leaves and edible flowers. Simple as that!

½ tsp orange blossom water

1 tsp lemon juice

1 tbsp extra virgin olive oil

½ tsp each unrefined salt and cracked white pepper

1   Place the orange blossom water and lemon juice in a small bowl, then slowly whisk in the oil until emulsified. Season, then taste and adjust if necessary. This dressing will last in the fridge for at least 2 weeks.

VARIATIONS

✔ Add:
  1 tsp pomegranate molasses.
  1 tsp raw honey or rice syrup.

✔ Use blood orange or grapefruit juice instead of lemon juice.

LEMONY QUARK SAUCE

GF V SF NF GrF R

This is a versatile little number and I suggest using it with quite a few recipes in this book – Poached veggies (page 120), Sweet potato fritters (page 110), Roast veggies (page 102), Fantastic veggie fritters (page 28), Ancient grains (page 130) and Moroccan pumpkin and chickpea casserole (page 98). Its subtle lemon taste brings out the flavour in other foods so well. Quark is a fermented dairy product that is high in protein and great for your digestion and immune system.

260 g (9¼ oz/1 cup) quark or plain yoghurt

2 tbsp olive oil

grated zest and juice of 1 lemon or 1 tsp finely chopped preserved lemon

1 tbsp each finely chopped coriander and flat-leaf parsley

½ tsp each unrefined salt and cracked white pepper

1   Combine all the ingredients in a bowl or blitz in a food processor or blender and blitz until smooth and creamy. Store in an airtight container in the fridge for up to a week.

BABA GHANOUSH WITH POMEGRANATE SEEDS

GF V SF NF GrF

This dip is just so Middle Eastern. The pomegranate seeds, like little rubies sitting on top, give it a lovely tang and the sheep's yoghurt, a creamy finish. Pomegranates are a winter fruit and are known in Ayurvedic medicine to reduce phlegm. They're also highly prized for being anti-carcinogenic (anti-cancer). Eat this with my Flatbread (page 134), Roast veggies (page 102) and Chopped salad with black beans and pomegranate molasses (page 30).

1 large eggplant

2 tbsp hulled tahini

2 tbsp lemon juice

2 garlic cloves, crushed

1 tsp unrefined salt

2 tbsp chopped flat-leaf parsley

95 g (3¼ oz/⅓ cup) sheep's yoghurt

2 tbsp pomegranate seeds (when in season)

1 Preheat your oven to 200°C (400°F/Gas 6).

2 Place your eggplant on a baking tray and pierce it about six times with a small sharp knife. Pop in the oven and bake for about 30 minutes until collapsed and soft. Allow to cool.

3 Scoop out the eggplant flesh, then roughly chop and place in a bowl. Use a fork to mash it quite well, then add the tahini, lemon juice, garlic, salt, parsley and yoghurt. Mix well or transfer to a food processor or blender and blitz, then pour into a bowl to serve. If you have them, sprinkle the pomegranate seeds on top.

VARIATIONS

✓ Leave the yoghurt out for a vegan dip.

✓ Serve with All seed crackers (page 150).

TEMPEH AND SWEET POTATO CROUTONS

GF DF VG V NF GrF

Sprinkle these croutons on salads, noodles, steamed veggies or soups.

185 g (6½ oz/1 cup) cubed tempeh

140 g (5 oz/1 cup) diced sweet potato

2 tsp macadamia oil

2 tsp sesame oil

1 tbsp tamari

75 g (2¾ oz/½ cup) toasted sesame seeds

1 Preheat your oven to 200°C (400°F/Gas 6).

2 In a shallow bowl, mix together the tempeh and sweet potato, then add the oils, tamari and sesame seeds. Transfer to a baking tray and bake, stirring a couple of times to ensure an even colour, for 15–20 minutes until crispy. Serve immediately.

DESSERT & SWEET THINGS

CACAO AND COCONUT CRACKLES

GF DF VG V SF NF

These take just a few minutes to mix together and get into the fridge, and are an easy and nutritious after-school snack or kids' party treat. What am I talking about? These are great for grown-ups or kids at any time.

125 ml (4 fl oz/½ cup) coconut oil

17 g (½ oz/½ cup) desiccated or shredded coconut

55 g (2 oz/½ cup) raw cacao powder

45 g (1½ oz/1½ cups) puffed rice or millet

75 g (2¾ oz/½ cup) currants

1 tbsp syrup sweetener

1   Melt the oil (if it has solidified) in a small saucepan over low heat, then pour into a bowl to cool a little.

2   Add the coconut, cacao powder, puffed grains, currants and sweetener, and stir well to combine. Spoon this mixture into 12 small patty cases, then pop into the fridge for about 30 minutes, or the freezer for 10 minutes, until set. Store in the fridge or freezer for up to 3 months.

VARIATIONS

✔ Add 60 g (2¼ oz/½ cup) chopped pecans to the mix.

✔ Any puffed grains will be fine.

ROASTED HAZELNUT AND COFFEE CHOCOLATE CUPS

GF DF VG V SF GrF

Once you know the basics of making your own chocolate, then the options for flavours are endless, plus you have the benefit of knowing exactly what's gone into it. No more palm oil, milk solids, refined sugar and cacao beans using child labour. Only natural, sustainable and ethical ingredients. These delicious chocolates are pictured on page 176.

125 ml (4 fl oz/½ cup) coconut oil, warmed

80 g (2¾ oz/¾ cup) raw cacao powder

90 g (3¼ oz/½ cup) syrup sweetener

pinch of unrefined salt

1½ tbsp espresso coffee

2 tbsp toasted and roughly chopped hazelnuts, extra to serve

1 Beat all the ingredients together until combined. Put 12 tiny patty cases in a muffin tray and fill with the chocolate mixture. Garnish with extra nuts, if using. Place in the freezer for about 10 minutes to set. Serve and eat. Store them in the freezer for up to 2 months.

VARIATIONS

✓ For Jaffa cups, leave out the coffee and nuts and fill the patty cases to only one-third. Mix together 125 ml (4 fl oz/½ cup) warm coconut oil, 3 tbsp orange juice, 1 tbsp grated orange zest, 1 tsp natural vanilla extract and 2 tsp syrup or granule sweetener. Place 1 tbsp of this mixture on top of the chocolate base, then top with more of the chocolate mixture. Freeze for 15 or so minutes.

✓ Add ½ cup puffed rice or quinoa to the chocolate mixture before spooning into the patty cases for freezing.

POMEGRANATE AND ALMOND PANCAKES

GF DF V SF GrF

Pure pomegranate juice is packed with antioxidants, so try to find it.

2 eggs, lightly whisked

250 ml (9 fl oz/1 cup) almond milk

½ vanilla bean, split lengthways and seeds scraped

4 tbsp coconut nectar

200 g (7 oz/2 cups) almond meal

1 tsp baking powder

185 g (6½ oz/1½ cups) roughly chopped raspberries

3 tbsp coconut oil

raspberries and chopped almonds, to serve (optional)

POMEGRANATE SYRUP

250 ml (9 fl oz/1 cup) 100% pure pomegranate juice

1 tbsp coconut nectar

1 Preheat the oven to 160°C (315°F/Gas 2–3).

2 In a small bowl, whisk together the eggs, almond milk, vanilla seeds and coconut nectar. In a separate bowl, mix together the almond meal and baking powder. Make a well in the centre and gradually add the wet ingredients to the dry, stirring slowly. Mix until the batter is smooth, then add the chopped raspberries.

3 Heat some of the coconut oil in a frying pan over medium heat. Using a ladle, pour in 60 ml (2 fl oz/ ¼ cup) of the batter and tilt the pan to evenly distribute it. Cook for a couple of minutes until air bubbles form on the surface. Flip the pancake and cook the other side for 1–3 minutes until golden. Place on a plate and keep covered with a clean tea towel. Repeat with the remaining coconut oil and batter.

4 For the pomegranate syrup, pour the pomegranate juice into a small saucepan and bring to the boil. Reduce the heat to low, add the nectar and simmer without stirring for about 15 minutes until reduced and thick and syrupy. Remove from the heat.

5 Serve the pancakes with the raspberries and chopped almonds, if you like, and a generous drizzle of pomegranate syrup.

VARIATIONS

✓ Serve with 130 g (4¾ oz/½ cup) quark or sheep's yoghurt.

✓ Use any syrup sweetener in place of the coconut nectar.

BANANA NUT CUPCAKES

DF V SF

Yummy little cakes.

150 g (5 oz/1 cup) wholemeal spelt flour

150 g (5 oz/1 cup) spelt flour

3 tsp baking powder

1 tbsp chia seeds

110 g (4 oz/½ cup) granule sweetener

2 tbsp peanut butter or nut butter

185 ml (6 fl oz/¾ cup) coconut or macadamia oil

240 g (8½ oz/1 cup) mashed banana (about 2 large bananas)

2 eggs, lightly whisked

170 ml (5½ fl oz/⅔ cup almond milk

1 Preheat your oven to 200°C (400°F/Gas 6). Grease a 12-hole muffin tin.

2 In a bowl, sift together the flours and baking powder, then add the chia seeds and sweetener and mix well.

3 In a separate bowl, combine the peanut or nut butter, oil, banana, eggs and almond milk. Mix the wet and dry ingredients together until just combined. Do not overmix. Spoon the mixture into the prepared tin, filling each muffin hole two-thirds full. Bake for 20 minutes or until golden.

4 Cool the cupcakes in the tin for 5 minutes, then turn out and cool on a wire rack. Store in an airtight container for up to 1 week or freeze for up to 3 months.

VARIATIONS

✓ If you'd like a nut-free version, replace the nut butter with tahini.

✓ For something a bit decadent, slather Chocolate coconut spread (page 167) on top of the cooled cupcakes.

✓ Add ½ cup cacao nibs with the flour.

STEWED NUTTY FRUIT

GF V SF GrF

This lovely stewed fruit is gorgeous over yoghurt with chopped nuts, coconut ice cream or just on its own.

2 apples, cored and sliced

2 pears, cored and sliced

2 peaches, stones removed, sliced

1 cinnamon stick

1 star anise

½ tsp ground cloves or 2 whole cloves

grated zest and juice of 1 orange

40 g (1½ oz/⅓ cup) roughly chopped
   raw unsalted pistachio nuts

3 tbsp water

260 g (9¼ oz/1 cup) plain yoghurt

1 tbsp LSA

1 tbsp hemp seeds

1 tbsp syrup or granule sweetener
   (optional)

1 Place the fruit in a saucepan with the cinnamon, star anise, cloves, orange zest and juice, pistachios and water and cook over medium–low heat for 10 minutes or until the fruit is tender.

2 Serve warm in small bowls with a dollop of the yoghurt, a sprinkle of the LSA and hemp seeds and a drizzle of the sweetener of your choice.

VARIATIONS

✔ For a dairy-free or vegan option, use coconut yoghurt.

✔ Use quark instead of the yoghurt.

✔ Add some chia seeds to the garnish.

✔ For the flavour of a Christmas mince tart, try it with organic dried fruit such as raisins, currants, dates, sultanas and/or dried cranberries.

COCONUT CREPES

GF DF V SF NF

I realise these sound a bit fancy and complicated, but they are no more so than any crepe. They are something a bit special. Have them rolled up ready to go for dessert after a dinner party. You don't have to fry them, but, OMG, I would.

2 tbsp coconut oil, plus extra for frying the crepes

1 tsp cardamom seeds

100 g (3½ oz/1½ cups) shredded, young coconut

4 tbsp coconut palm sugar, plus extra to serve

pinch of unrefined salt

COCONUT CREPES

160 g (5¾ oz/1 cup) white rice or other gluten-free flour

2 tbsp tapioca flour or gluten-free cornflour

2 eggs, lightly whisked

1 tbsp coconut oil

about 375 ml (13 fl oz/1½ cups) water

pinch of unrefined salt

1 Heat the oil in a saucepan over medium heat, then pop in the cardamom seeds and cook for a few seconds until fragrant. Add the coconut, sugar and salt, reduce the heat to low and stir for a few minutes until the coconut is a gorgeous golden brown. Set aside to cool.

2 Meanwhile, make the crepes. Sift the two flours together into a bowl and make a well in the centre. Pour in the eggs and oil and, whisking constantly, gradually pour in the water until a smooth batter forms. Add the salt and whisk again, then rest for 30 minutes.

3 Heat a heavy-based frying pan or crepe pan over medium heat and, using a pastry brush or some paper towel, wipe a little of the extra oil over the base of the pan. Use a ladle or jug to pour about 80 ml (2½ fl oz/⅓ cup) of the batter into the pan, tilting as you go to evenly distribute it. Reduce the heat to low and cook for about 1 minute until the batter sets and lifts at the edges, then flip and cook until the underside just changes colour. Lift the crepe onto a plate, cover with a tea towel to keep warm or pop it into a 100°C (200°F/Gas ½) oven. Repeat with extra oil and the remaining batter.

4 To assemble, place a crepe on a work surface and heap 1–2 tablespoons of the coconut mixture near the edge closest to you. Fold this edge over the filling, tuck in the sides and roll up to form a log. Repeat until all the pancakes and filling have been used.

5 Serve as is or heat an oiled frying pan and fry the crepes in batches, sprinkling with a little extra sugar towards the end of the cooking, until golden and sticky on all sides.

BARBECUED PINEAPPLE

GF V SF NF GrF

It's always a bit of a struggle thinking about what to have for dessert after a barbie. Here's the answer.

1 tbsp coconut oil

1 small pineapple, skin and core removed, cut into long wedges

2 tbsp coconut palm sugar

2 tbsp kirsch or dark rum

8 mint leaves, shredded

1 tbsp raw cacao powder

260 g (9¼ oz/1 cup) plain yoghurt, quark or coconut ice cream

1   Heat the oil in a frying pan over medium heat, add the pineapple and cook, sprinkling on the sugar, for about 3–4 minutes or until golden brown on each side. Drizzle on the kirsch or rum and cook for another minute, until the syrup is thick. Transfer to a platter and sprinkle on the mint and cacao powder. Serve with the yoghurt, quark or ice cream.

VARIATIONS

✓ Use cacao nibs instead of the cacao powder or leave out the cacao altogether.

✓ You can also use mango cheeks or bananas cut in half lengthways, leaving the skin on both to hold them together.

TAHINI AND DATE FUDGE

GF DF VG V SF NF GrF

A two-ingredient, foolproof sweet. Now we're talking. Tahini is a great source of essential fatty acids, calcium and protein. Use hulled or unhulled but know that the latter has a stronger, nuttier taste and a darker colour.

540 g (1 lb 3 oz/2 cups) hulled tahini

320 g (11¼ oz/2 cups) pitted and roughly chopped dates

1   Place the tahini and dates in a food processor and blitz until thick and chunky. Press into a 20-cm × 20-cm (8-in × 8-in) square baking paper-lined cake tin, cover and pop into the freezer for 2 hours until almost firm.

2   Cut the fudge into bite-sized squares and then put back into the freezer for another hour until firm.

VARIATIONS

✔ Add:
a few drops of natural vanilla extract.
½ cup walnuts and/or cacao nibs.

VELVET CUPCAKES WITH CASHEW FROSTING

DF VG V SF

Not only do these look incredible, but they taste amazing.

3 beetroot, steamed or boiled, peeled and roughly chopped

3 tbsp coconut sweetener

4 tbsp coconut oil, melted

2 eggs

2 tsp lemon juice

1 tsp natural vanilla extract or 1 vanilla bean, split in half lengthways and seeds scraped

195 g (7 oz/1¼ cups) spelt flour

2 tbsp raw cacao powder

1 tsp baking powder

¼ tsp unrefined salt

FROSTING

155 g (5½ oz/1 cup) raw cashews, soaked in water for a few hours or overnight

1 tsp natural vanilla extract

2 tbsp granule sweetener

2 tsp lemon juice

1   Preheat your oven to 175°C (345°F/Gas 4) and line 2 × 6-hole muffin tins with patty cases.

2   Blitz the beetroot in a food processor until smooth, then add the sweetener, coconut oil, eggs, lemon juice and vanilla and process until smooth. Set aside.

3   In a large bowl, whisk together the dry ingredients.

4   Pour the beetroot mixture into the dry ingredients and mix until just combined. Spoon the batter into the prepared muffin holes and bake for 20 minutes until a toothpick or skewer inserted in the centre of a cupcake comes out clean. Let cool a little before turning out onto a wire rack to cool completely.

5   For the frosting, drain the cashews and place in a food processor. Add the vanilla, sweetener and lemon juice and whiz until very smooth. If necessary, add a little water to get it to a smooth consistency. Chill for about an hour so it becomes nice and stiff.

6   Using a spatula or piping bag, top the cupcakes with the frosting. Store in the fridge in an airtight container for up to 3–5 days.

VARIATION

✔ If you want to have crumbles on top of your frosting, reserve one cupcake and don't ice it. Instead, crumble it into a bowl and, once you are done frosting the other cupcakes, sprinkle the crumbs on top.

STRAWBERRY MOUSSE

GF DF VG V SF NF GrF R

This recipe keeps well in the fridge. Make up a large batch for the week ahead so that you aren't caught out when sugar cravings strike.

2 cups frozen strawberries

1 × 200 ml (7 fl oz) BPA-free tin coconut milk

2 tbsp chia seeds

1 tbsp maca powder

2 dates

80 g (2¾ oz/½ cup) blueberries

30 g (1 oz/⅓ cup) coconut flakes

1   Combine the strawberries, coconut milk, chia seeds, maca powder and dates in your blender or food processor and blitz until smooth. Pour into glass jars of about 250 ml (9 fl oz/1 cup) capacity then sprinkle with a few blueberries and some coconut. Secure with a lid or cover. These will keep in the fridge for a week.

BANANA AND TAHINI ICE CREAM

GF DF VG V SF NF GrF

This is perfect when you have that little hankering for something sweet at night.

1 frozen banana

2 tsp hulled tahini

1 tsp grated lemon zest

1 tsp water

1 Toss all the ingredients in a blender, then whiz for a few seconds until smooth and thick. Serve at once.

VARIATIONS

✔ Add:
  1 tbsp raw cacao powder or cacao nibs.
  1 chopped softened date.

CHIA AND BERRY JAM

GF DF VG V SF NF GrF R

This yummy spread contains loads of antioxidants, protein, vitamin A and omega 3, and it's raw, gluten-, sugar-, nut- and dairy-free and vegan. Perfecto! Serve with Sikarni (page 190). Also try this on toast with a slathering of macadamia butter, or on yoghurt or ice cream.

1 cup blackberries, blueberries, strawberries or mulberries (frozen organic is fine)

1 tbsp chia seeds

1 tbsp warm water

1 tbsp syrup sweetener

1   Place everything in a food processor and whiz until combined.

VARIATIONS

✔ Add:
1 tbsp date paste (available from health food stores or delis), or 2 fresh dates to the above ingredients.

1 tsp natural vanilla extract or the seeds from a split vanilla bean.

1 tsp lemon or orange juice and the grated zest.

CHERRY RIPE

GF DF VG V NF SF GrF R

These healthy sweets take only a few minutes to prepare and less than 30 minutes to set. They're great to have in the freezer when someone pops around, for a dinner party or just for you when you feel like something sweet. Get rid of the chocolate biscuits full of palm oil, trans fats, white sugar and flour in the pantry and fill your freezer with medicinal life-extending chocolate.

BASE

1 cup shredded or desiccated coconut

125 ml (4 fl oz/½ cup) coconut oil

¼ cup frozen cherries

1 tbsp syrup or granule sweetener

TOPPING

30 g (1 oz/¼ cup) raw cacao powder

2 tbsp coconut oil

1 vanilla bean, split in half lengthways and seeds scraped

1   Line a 20-cm × 20-cm (8-in × 8-in) cake tin with baking paper.

2   For the base, place the coconut, oil, cherries and sweetener in your food processor and process until well combined. Press into the prepared cake tin and pop in the freezer for an hour.

3   For the topping, place the cacao powder in a heatproof bowl over a saucepan of hot water. Add the oil and vanilla, stirring, and allow to melt.

4   Pour the chocolate topping over the cherry base and place in the fridge to set for 20 minutes before you slice it into small pieces, using a warm, dry knife.

VARIATION

✓ Add some syrup or granule sweetener to the topping if you like. About 2 tsp should do it.

COCONUT-BANANA POPSICLES

GF DF VG V NF SF GrF R

A lovely easy iceblock recipe for the warmer months. Use whatever fruit you have in abundance.

1 × 200 ml (7 fl oz) BPA-free tin coconut milk

1 banana

35 g (1¼ oz/½ cup) shredded coconut

1 tbsp lime juice

2 tbsp syrup or granule sweetener (optional)

1 Combine everything in a blender and blend until smooth. Pour into iceblock moulds and freeze until firm, about 4 hours.

VARIATIONS

✔ Use mango, pineapple, dragonfruit, berries or passionfruit instead of the banana.

✔ Add 1 tsbp chia seeds for a hit of calcium and omega oils.

BUCKWHEAT AND CACAO PANCAKES WITH GANACHE

DF VG V SF

These chocolatey pancakes hold together very well. Using a 'flax egg' instead of an egg really does the trick. You can also use chia seeds instead of flax if you like.

65 g (2½ oz/½ cup) buckwheat flour

¼ cup oat flour

1¼ tsp baking powder

¼ tsp bicarbonate of soda

pinch of unrefined salt

1 tbsp raw cacao powder

3 tbsp raw beetroot juice

3 tbsp non-dairy milk

2 tbsp granule sweetener

1 tsp natural vanilla extract

1 tbsp coconut oil

mangoes, strawberries, passionfruit or blueberries, to serve

FLAX EGG

1 tsp flaxseed meal

2–3 tsp warm water

GANACHE

55 g (2 oz/½ cup) raw cacao powder

185 ml (6 fl oz/¾ cup) coconut oil

2 tbsp cacao butter

few drops of natural vanilla extract

1–2 tbsp syrup or granule sweetener (optional)

1   To make the flax egg, in a small bowl, mix the flaxseed meal with the warm water and set aside to gel.

2   In a large bowl, mix together the dry ingredients.

3   In another bowl, whisk together the beetroot juice, milk, sweetener, vanilla and flax egg.

4   Add the wet ingredients to the dry ingredients and mix until thick and just combined.

5   Heat about 1 teaspoon of the coconut oil in a heavy-based frying pan over medium–low heat. Pour one-quarter of the batter into the pan, tilting it to distribute the batter evenly. Cook for 2–3 minutes, until bubbles appear, then flip and cook for another minute. They should feel firm to the touch. Place on a plate and cover with a tea towel. Repeat with the remaining oil and batter. You should get about 6 medium-sized pancakes.

6   To make the ganache, place a heatproof bowl over a saucepan of simmering water, add the cacao powder, oil, cacao butter and vanilla, and stir until melted and smooth. Adjust the consistency by adding more oil or butter, if you like, and add some sweetener, if you think it needs it.

7   To serve, place a couple of pancakes on each plate and pour the ganache over the top of the pancakes. Serve with the fruit.

VARIATION

✔ For gluten-free pancakes, try using brown rice flour.

PISTACHIO, FIG AND STRAWBERRY 'CHEESECAKE'

GF DF VG V SF GrF R

This is a very simple, foolproof and fast recipe to put together. Plus it tastes amazing, and it's loaded with nutrients in their raw state. Clearly it's not a traditional cheesecake using cream cheese, sugar and eggs, but it has a similar texture and playfulness about it.

BASE

155 g (5½ oz/1 cup) each cashew nuts and macadamia nuts, soaked in water for 2 hours, then drained

4 dried figs, soaked in water for 1 hour in 375 ml (13 fl oz/1½ cups) water, then drained (keep liquid)

½ tsp freshly grated nutmeg

FILLING

225 g (8 oz/1½ cups) raw unsalted pistachio nuts, soaked in water for 2 hours then drained

4 tbsp syrup sweetener

2 tsp psyllium husks

2 tsp lecithin granules, non-GMO

grated zest and juice of ½ lemon

1 vanilla bean, split in half lengthways and seeds scraped

pinch of unrefined salt

scant 4 tbsp coconut oil

TOPPING

300 g (10½ oz/2 cups) strawberries, trimmed

grated zest and juice of ½ lemon

1 tbsp syrup or granule sweetener (optional)

1 For the base, place the cashews, macadamias, figs and nutmeg in a food processor and blitz until combined. Press into a 23-cm (9-in) springform cake tin. Put it in the fridge to firm up while you're making the filling.

2 Place the soaking liquid from the figs in a blender or food processor, then add the syrup, pistachios, psyllium husks, lecithin, lemon zest and juice, vanilla seeds, salt and oil, and process until a thick purée forms. Pour this onto the base and smooth with a spatula, then pop back into the fridge for at least 4 hours or overnight.

3 For the topping, combine your berries with the lemon zest and juice and, if you want to use it, the sweetener in a blender or food processor and whiz until combined. Serve in a jug on the side.

VARIATION

✓ Use dates, prunes or frozen berries in the topping instead of strawberries.

RAW BEAUTY PROTEIN LOG

GF DF VG V SF GrF R

Packed with goodness, watch your skin start to glow as you chew on one of these bars.

½ cup dried fruit (such as goji berries, figs, dates, cranberries or raisins)

2 tbsp chia seeds

2 tbsp hemp seeds

¼ cup flaxseed meal

25 g (1 oz/⅓ cup) shredded coconut

55 g (2 oz/⅓ cup) whole almonds

½ tsp ground cinnamon

3 tbsp water

1 Place the dried fruit in a bowl, cover with water and soak for 30–60 minutes, then drain.

2 Combine all the ingredients in a food processor and blitz until you get a smooth, shiny paste.

3 Spoon the paste onto a sheet of baking paper and shape into a long, thin log, about 20 cm × 5 cm (8 in × 2 in). Wrap the paper firmly around the log, squeezing as you go. Twist the ends to secure and pop into the fridge for 2–3 minutes until firm. Slice into 2-cm (¾-in) pieces to serve. Keep the log in the paper in the fridge for up to 2 weeks.

SPICED GINGER COOKIES

GF DF VG V NF SF

Truly a great cookie, and one of the most popular recipes on my Facebook page. These little mouthfuls of spice heaven are quick and easy to make, and they'll freeze well also. To make these suitable for school lunches, replace the almond meal with a flour such as brown rice flour or even coconut flour.

250 g (9 oz/2½ cups) almond meal

210 g (7½ oz/1¼ cups) pitted dates

1 tsp baking soda

pinch of unrefined salt

2 tbsp coconut oil

1 egg

1 tsp natural vanilla extract

1 tsp ground cinnamon

1½ tsp ground ginger

½ tsp freshly grated nutmeg

½ tsp ground cloves

1   Preheat your oven to 175°C (345°F/Gas 4). In a food processor pulse 1½ cups of the almond meal then pulse the dates separately. You don't want a paste, so be careful not to overprocess. Combine them and put back in the processor with the rest of the almond meal and remaining ingredients. Pulse until a ball is formed.

2   Roll into walnut-sized balls and place on a tray. Flatten a little with a fork then bake for about 15 minutes or until just starting to become a nice golden brown.

VARIATIONS

✓ Use brown rice flour or any other gluten-free flour to keep them both gluten- and nut-free.

✓ Add ½ cup cacao nibs or powder.

DRINKS

MILK

DF VG V SF R

These days we're drinking all sorts of different milks, and many of us aren't drinking any cow's milk at all. It really is so easy and quick to make your own milk at home. All you need is a good blender – and to be prepared for less packaging and sugar at your place and more money in your wallet. So start experimenting and vary your milk from day to day, recipe to recipe. Soak your base overnight for an easier blend.

750 ml (26 fl oz/3 cups) water

BASE

1 cup of the base (seeds – hemp, pepitas, sesame or sunflower seeds or quinoa; any type of nut – almond, cashew, macadamia, Brazil, hazelnut; grains, such as oats or brown rice; coconut – use desiccated or flesh from young fruit)

1 Cover your base in water and soak overnight.

2 The next day, drain your base (I use the water on my plants), then pop into the blender with the water and blend until smooth. You can use the milk just like this, with the pulp, or strain it through a piece of muslin or a fine sieve. Don't discard the pulp. You can use it to add to biscuits, cakes, pancakes and curries. If making coconut milk, use the pulp again. Cover with water for about an hour, then blitz again in your blender then strain. This is called 'second milk'.

3 The milk will last for 3–4 days in an airtight container in the fridge.

VARIATIONS

✔ Add:
   1 tsp natural vanilla extract or the seeds from a split vanilla bean.
   1 tsp lemon juice.
   1 tsp syrup sweetener.

✔ You can use fresh coconut flesh instead of dried.

MANGO, CHIA AND LIME SMOOTHIE

GF DF VG V SF NF GrF R

This is a pretty nice way to start the day. The chia seeds are a great source of protein to kickstart your brain, and a really good plant source of calcium. They're also wonderful for helping balance your blood sugar – keeping you feeling full for longer.

250 ml (9 fl oz/1 cup) coconut water, chilled

1 frozen mango cheek

1 tsp chia seeds

1 tsp flaxseed oil

1 tsp grated lime zest

1 tsp syrup sweetener (optional)

1   Combine all the ingredients, sweetening as you like, in a blender and blitz until smooth. Serve in a tall glass.

VARIATIONS

✓ Use any type of milk instead of the coconut water.

✓ Add 1 tsp coconut or flaxseed oil.

MILKSHAKE

GF DF VG V SF GrF R

Most people love the idea of a milkshake. But many of us are lactose intolerant, plus there's so much sugar and goodness knows what else in that syrup. As usual, my advice is to make your own. The maca powder replaces the malt of yesteryear. What a gorgeous thing to serve unexpected guests, or for something different besides tea and coffee.

750 ml (26 fl oz/3 cups) dairy-free milk

1 tsp syrup sweetener

1 tsp maca powder

1 tsp raw cacao powder

1   Pop all the ingredients into a blender and blitz until combined and fluffy.

VARIATIONS

✓ For a strawberry milkshake, omit the cacao powder and add 75 g (2¾ oz/½ cup) strawberries that you've blended with a little water, then strained.

✓ For a vanilla milkshake, omit the cacao powder, then add 1 tsp natural vanilla extract or the seeds from a split vanilla bean.

✓ For a mocha milkshake, leave the cacao powder in and add a 30 ml (1 fl oz) shot of espresso coffee.

MORNING LIVER SHOT

GF DF V SF NF GrF R

It's a lovely idea to start the day with lemon juice in warm water, as many of us do, but how about trying something with turmeric? Keep the water below boiling so as to keep the honey raw. You can make a big batch and keep it in the fridge so you can pour out a 30 ml (1 fl oz) shot each morning.

4 tbsp water
1 tbsp grated, then pounded, fresh turmeric
1 tsp raw honey

1   Bring the water almost to the boil in a kettle. In a small glass, combine the turmeric and honey, then add the water and stir.

VARIATION
✓   Use any complex sweetener.

COFFEE AND COCONUT MOCKTAIL

GF DF VG V SF NF GrF

For a seductive non-alcoholic special drink, go no further. Or go ahead and add a splash of frangelico.

250 ml (9 fl oz/1 cup) coconut water, chilled
½ cup frozen mango chunks
1½ tbsp espresso coffee, chilled
1 tsp grated lime zest
1 tsp–1 tbsp syrup or granule sweetener

1   Combine all the ingredients, sweetening as you like, in a blender and blend until smooth. Serve in a tall glass.

GINGER TEA

GF DF VG V SF NF GrF

This tea gets better with time, so if you make it in advance and reheat it when you want to serve it, you'll be very pleased with the intense flavour. Use a mandoline or vegetable peeler to get the slices nice and thin.

1 litre (35 fl oz/4 cups) water

5-cm (2-in) piece of fresh ginger, peeled and thinly sliced

1 cinnamon stick

1 tsp black peppercorns

1 slice lemon peel, using a veggie peeler

2 tbsp coconut palm sugar

1 cup thinly sliced young coconut flesh

1   Place the water, ginger, cinnamon, peppercorns, lemon peel and sugar in a saucepan and bring to the boil, stirring until the sugar has dissolved. Continue to boil rapidly without stirring for a couple of minutes. Then reduce the heat to low and simmer for about 15 minutes until it has reduced a little.

2   Divide the coconut between four heatproof glasses and pour in the ginger tea. Serve with a long spoon to get the coconut out.

VARIATION

✓ Chill the tea, then strain and serve with ice.

ANTI-INFLAMMATORY SMOOTHIE

GF DF VG V SF NF GrF

Turmeric is great for your liver and heart and is a tasty way to reduce inflammation.

1 ripe banana

½ cup frozen mango chunks

250 ml (9 fl oz/1 cup) orange juice

1 tbsp coconut oil

2 tsp grated fresh ginger

1 tsp grated fresh turmeric

3 tbsp coconut milk

125 ml (4 fl oz/½ cup) water

1   Place the banana, mango, orange juice, coconut oil, ginger and turmeric in a blender and blend on high speed until smooth. Add the coconut milk and water and blend again to incorporate. Pour into two glasses and serve.

VARIATION
✔ Garnish with ½ tsp hemp seeds.

ALMOND AND CACAO NIGHTCAP

GF DF VG V SF GrF

Nuts are a great source of tryptophan, which induces sleep, and cacao is one of the best sources of magnesium. Having trouble sleeping? Make yourself a modern-day warm chocolate milk.

625 ml (21½ fl oz/2½ cups) almond milk

1 heaped tsp cashew or macadamia nut butter

1 tsp syrup sweetener

1 tsp raw cacao powder

1   Pour your milk into a small saucepan and gently heat over low heat until just simmering.

2   Divide the nut butter, sweetener and cacao powder between two mugs, then pour the hot milk over the top. Stir well to combine and adjust the sweetness to how you like it.

VARIATION
✔ For a richer drink, add 1 tsp cacao butter.

INDEX